Crossing That Foggy Bridge

...from pain to peace
...from depression to delight

Beverly Easler

WESTBOW
P R E S S®
A DIVISION OF THOMAS NELSON
& ZONDERVAN

WestBow Press books may be ordered through booksellers or by contacting:

WestBow Press
A Division of Thomas Nelson & Zondervan
1663 Liberty Drive
Bloomington, IN 47403
www.westbowpress.com
1 (866) 928-1240

Because of the dynamic nature of the Internet, any web addresses or links contained in this book may have changed since publication and may no longer be valid. The views expressed in this work are solely those of the author and do not necessarily reflect the views of the publisher, and the publisher hereby disclaims any responsibility for them.

Any people depicted in stock imagery provided by Getty Images are models, and such images are being used for illustrative purposes only. Certain stock imagery © Getty Images.

THE HOLY BIBLE, NEW INTERNATIONAL VERSION®, NIV® Copyright © 1973, 1978, 1984, 2011 by Biblica, Inc.® Used by permission. All rights reserved worldwide.

Scripture taken from the New Century Version®. Copyright © 2005 by Thomas Nelson. Used by permission. All rights reserved.

Scripture taken from The Message. Copyright © 1993, 1994, 1995, 1996, 2000, 2001, 2002. Used by permission of NavPress Publishing Group.

ISBN: 978-1-9736-6405-5 (sc)
ISBN: 978-1-9736-6406-2 (hc)
ISBN: 978-1-9736-6404-8 (e)

Library of Congress Control Number: 2019907009

Print information available on the last page.

WestBow Press rev. date: 6/20/2019

With Heartfelt Thanks

This book would not exist apart from the foggy bridges I've crossed over during multiple years of depression and self-defeat. More important, my hesitant and fearful steps onto those bridges would not have been attempted without the support and encouragement of family, friends, and counselors. Three noteworthy people have played enduring roles in my journey over the past twenty-five years. These God-provided helpers have consistently taught, encouraged, prodded, and comforted me in their own unique ways.

Connie Dummer, psychotherapist extraordinaire, encourager, and friend: With her constant patience, her knowledge, and her wisdom, Connie has stuck with me through my obstinance and painful silences, rejoiced in my tiny steps forward, and persistently reminded me of the healing presence of Jesus Christ.

Pastor Leith Anderson, current president of the National Association of Evangelicals: Through his eloquent and timely messages as well as his quiet, personal counsel, Leith has always presented the Truth to me, even when I didn't want to hear it.

Kathy Troccoli, Christian singer/songwriter: With her captivating voice, Kathy continues to provide those musical hugs I seek and cherish. Through her tender heart and transparent lyrics, she draws me ever closer to a complete understanding of the stubborn love of Jesus, "my husband, my Maker, my friend."

Thank you, Connie; thank you, Leith; and thank you, Kathy. Each of you has, with your own special gifts, reached through the fog of my pain and depression and faithfully led me to the Source of true peace and delight.

Thank you, Jesus, my One and Only, for placing these and other precious people in my path to lead me out of my darkness and into your Light.

Contents

Introduction

A chill wind blows across my soul;
my mind and heart have grown stone cold.
As I go trudging through the day,
my eyes see only shades of gray.
My ears won't hear, and darkness looms
as shame cloaks all my thoughts in gloom.
I'm sick from crying through the night.
I hate the dark but shun the light.
My heart is heavy like a stone,
and no one cares … I'm all alone.
—my journal

Depression is more than just being down in the dumps. It's more than a seasonal disorder that can be alleviated with a sun lamp. It's as different from the blues as a broken back is from a broken toe. Whether mental health professionals want to call depression a disease, a disorder, a condition, or simply a figment of the imagination is irrelevant to those of us who live with depression. Depression is *real.*

Depression is a dark place that can swallow you whole and drag you into a pit where there is no light or rest. It's a place that seems to control you with fear, self-loathing, and shame. You feel alone in your struggle, unnoticed in your pain, and unloved in your despair. The oppressive weight of depression can imprison and isolate you from your world, and it can hold you down for months, years, or a lifetime.

Through many dark, gloomy seasons of depression, I spent what seemed like thousands of hours and dollars on self-help books and psychotherapy, yet I often wondered why I even bothered. Although some of the things I learned from counselors and books did help, I was continually more confused and frustrated because every counselor and every author had a different approach to the problem.

Because depression has so many causes, so many ways of showing itself, and so many possible solutions, it's easy to get frustrated and give up on looking for answers. The search for help can become staggering and disheartening. If you go to the internet and type in the word *depression*, you'll find about 166 billion listings! You can't go shopping on Craigslist for a quick psychological makeover. You can't push a button on a vending machine and buy a package of peace. And there's certainly no phone number you can call to receive your instant, life-changing, depression zapper.

In spite of the massive resources available to anyone who can read a book, watch a video, or pay a therapist's fee, emotional pain and instability continue to wreak havoc in the lives of millions, young and old, rich and poor, single and married, including the Christian population.

I wish I could declare to you that I've found the secret formula for eliminating all depression and anxiety. If that were the case, I could package it and become a billionaire! Unfortunately, neither life nor depression comes with instructions. However, after years of research and counseling, I've been surprised to learn that 85 percent of all depression is a direct result of how we've learned to "do life."

We live in a broken world where there seems to be no right or wrong and no absolute truth for our human GPS to follow. We've been raised on the beliefs, morals, and behaviors of our families, and unless we were extremely fortunate, we often missed out on learning the skills needed to navigate the many demands that we encounter in the daily grind of life.

Through the patience and teaching of a wise counselor and the persistence and guidance of an even wiser God, I have found a way, through many frustrating trials and errors, to press on through life despite my depression and confusion. I have seen the impact of depression on my emotions, my thinking, and my relationships decrease significantly.

How? I've eradicated the self-defeating questions like "What's wrong with me?" and "Why am I so stupid?" and learned to ask better questions!

This book presents a series of questions related to many common problems we all face in life, including unending choices, faulty thinking, difficult relationship issues, fear and shame, and our beliefs about ourselves and the world we inhabit.

Although these questions are deliberately presented in a specific order, each chapter is written to stand alone. If you want to focus for some time on one question in the middle of the book, that's okay. However, I encourage you to read about each new question in sequence to bring you a logical step closer to a safe plank on that foggy bridge where you can safely sit and ponder before moving on to more challenging issues.

No matter how dark and hopeless your journey through life may seem, don't ever give up!

Life is a long, complicated process of sprinting and stumbling, laughing and crying, growing and changing. Doing life often hurts and saps your strength. Yet there is a wonderful Teacher and Savior named Jesus who has promised to walk with you and light the way ahead for as long as the process takes. "Never will I leave you; never will I forsake you" (Hebrews 13:5). According to 2 Corinthians 3:17-18, the ultimate goal of Jesus is that, through your growing knowledge of and maturity in Him, you will be transformed into His likeness!

Are you ready to move forward across that dark bridge of depression? Just reach for Jesus' hand, draw in a deep breath, close your eyes if you need to, and take that first uncertain step into the adventure of a lifetime.

Crossing that foggy bridge
... from pain to peace
... from depression to delight.

Chapter 1

Through the Fog

The fog closed in on me so slowly that I barely noticed it. There was only a hint of the fog at first: a subtle dimming of the already dusky sunlight, and some light moisture on the windshield. Soon the fog wrapped all around me like some evil mist in a horror movie. The headlights of the car behind me became an unwelcome intrusion as they pressed close and penetrated my rear window. Their cheery appearance seemed to be mocking my cautious progress through the murky sea of fog that drowned out the daylight. I felt dreadfully confined as a thick white curtain pressed against the car, and I entered a dark expanse of nothingness. I had no idea how deep the lake was under the bridge I was crossing. All I could think about was the very real possibility of becoming disoriented and going over the edge.

Frightened by that haunting thought, I almost screamed when the startling red eyes and ghostly silhouette of a gray wolf materialized out of nowhere. My heart beat furiously as my hands gripped the steering wheel so hard they turned white—the same pale shade as my face in that moment. I focused my eyes as best I could and concentrated on simply getting to the other end of the bridge and away from that red-eyed monster. Where did he come from? Was he really there, or was he just a figment of my overanxious imagination?

Depression can feel a lot like driving in the blinding whiteness of a thick fog. Your perspective on life's directions becomes blurred and can bewilder and frighten you. You get thrown off course by the expectations and demands of the people in your life, financial or medical issues, devastating losses or tragedies, and other circumstances beyond your control. The cheerfulness of others around you seems to taunt you, driving you deeper into despair as you slowly crawl through the oppressive darkness of your mind. The dark curtain of hopelessness envelops you until you're walled in, alienated from your friends, and no longer enjoying the activities that used to give you pleasure. The daily routine of life becomes difficult at best and devoid of meaning at its worst.

Why So Downcast?

Feeling defeated by life and groaning under the weight of depression is as old as the Bible. We live in a fallen world, and the reality of depression was true even for these Bible characters.

- Naomi: "My life is much too sad for you to share, because the Lord has been against me." (Ruth 1:13 NCV)
- Solomon: "Useless! Useless! Completely useless! Everything is useless." (Ecclesiastes 1:2 NCV)
- Job: "I don't have the strength to wait. There is nothing to hope for, so why should I be patient?" (Job 6:11 NCV)
- Elijah: "I have had enough Lord. Let me die. I am no better than my ancestors." (1 Kings 19:4 NCV)
- David: "My life is full of troubles, and I am nearly dead ... You have taken away my loved ones and friends. Darkness is my only friend." (Psalm 88:3, 18 NCV)
- Even Jesus said: "My soul is overwhelmed with sorrow to the point of death." (Mark 14:34 NCV)

One of the complications of depression is that it's so difficult to pinpoint the reasons for it. Sometimes you don't even recognize them because they could just as easily be symptoms associated with any bad day or bad mood.

- When you can't explain your depressed feelings, you blame a chemical imbalance, out-of-whack hormones, or lack of sleep.
- When you can't explain your bitter attitudes and quick temper, you blame money problems, the gloomy atmosphere at work, or that rude store clerk who refused to look at you.

- When you can't explain your self-destructive behavior, you blame it on poor self-esteem, that crazy driver who cut in front of you on the freeway, or some yet undiscovered childhood trauma that's damaged you in some way.
- You become desperately needy and clingy, depending on others to soothe your confused emotions and help you pretend you're okay.
- You feel more and more inadequate and incompetent and unlovable, and you begin to withdraw from life.
- Or you simply cop out by saying, "That's just the way I am."

When you can only guess at explanations for your depression or anxious hysterics, you plunge into a downward spiral as you begin the "If only" dirge.

- If only I were more like my sister.
- If only I were smarter.
- If only I had more money.
- If only I weren't so tired.
- If only I had some talent.
- If only my husband would change.
- If only I had a husband.

Your whining and blaming causes you to feel worse and throw your own little pity parties. The unfortunate result can be that those people who are most important to you start to turn their backs and walk away because they don't understand why you're suddenly striking out at them or manipulating them to take care of you.

Then you get mad at God. You think that because He's the one who made you this way, He should be doing something to help. "If God is against me, then there's really no hope! I might as well just give up!" At some point, you become so discouraged that you stop dead in your tracks and weep. It's easy to convince yourself that your particular crisis is unique, unlike anything ever experienced in the whole history of the world.

Although many of the books and articles I've read over the years have offered helpful information about the signs, symptoms, and treatments for depression, that information couldn't prepare me for the potholes, obstacles, and red-eyed monsters I've continued to encounter.

People around us who haven't experienced the empty, dark feeling of depression can't begin to understand how debilitating it can be. They think that people who claim they're depressed are simply wallowing in self-pity or using depression as an excuse for weakness. They believe we should be able to pull ourselves together and snap out of it. All we need to do is pop out of bed, swallow a pill, pray more, talk to a therapist or two, and jump back into an active and productive life. In protest against such counsel, one greeting card declared, "If people were meant to pop up, we'd all live in toasters!"

Depression can be especially difficult for Christians. There's rarely a class called Depression 101 in the curriculums of our churches or Christian colleges. Well-meaning friends in this "fellowship of the flawed" can unknowingly throw the depressed person under the bus with their implications that depression is proof of personal sin or an absence of faith. "Christians aren't supposed to be depressed," they say. "Where's that joy of the Lord you're supposed to feel?"

Those who've been imprisoned and crushed by depression have no answer to these unsympathetic and judgmental comments, having already passed judgment on themselves as flawed, unlovable, pathetic individuals. One of the most dismissive and belittling suggestions I heard was, "Try doing something for someone else who's worse off than you are."

When confronted with this kind of plastic advice, I would force myself to hide my tears and get busy "doing the Lord's work" so that I'd look strong and put together. Or I would simply walk away from the church for a time because I felt invisible, like that elephant in the pew no one wants to see or acknowledge. The silence of the Church regarding depression easily convinced me that even God couldn't possibly love me.

Trying Too Hard

There are so many who try to care
    and to understand when I hurt inside,
    but I think they try too hard.
They press me on all sides with their questions,
    attempting to make me share feelings
    that simply have no words.

They try to console me, thinking they're saying
    all the right words to soothe my mind
    and to make the ache in my heart less intense.
They try to wipe away my falling tears,
    almost as though they believe that
    once the tears are gone, the pain will vanish too.
They try so hard to say and do all the right things,
    not realizing that their efforts are only causing me
    to withdraw further into myself.
    If only they wouldn't try so hard. If only they knew
    that all I need is the warmth and comfort
    of their silence and compassion.

Wouldn't it be great if we could sit down with God's Word and quickly discover and apply His answers to the deep agony of our lives? We may find some measure of comfort and encouragement in familiar passages of scripture, such as Psalm 23:1–2, that speak to our personal pain.

The Lord is my shepherd, I shall not be in want. He makes me lie down in green pastures, he leads me beside quiet waters, he restores my soul.

Then we read verses like Ephesians 4:31–32, which exhort us to "Get rid of all bitterness, rage and anger, brawling and slander, along with every form of malice. Be kind and compassionate to one another, forgiving each other, just as in Christ God forgave you." We think, *Oh, sure, that sounds good, but how does that work for me? My coworkers treat me like dirt, my teenager hates me, my finances are a disaster, and my husband expects me to be Supermom!* We simply don't know how to turn those words of instruction into practical applications for the daily grind of life.

The mass media bombards us with advertisements about new miracle products and procedures along with testimonials from consumers who claim they've tried it and "It changed my life!" Yeah, right. Maybe some new dental procedure has resulted in a prettier smile and less embarrassment, or some hardware company has come up with a new, easier-to-use tool. But changed their lives? Not likely. If those consumers were depressed before, they're probably still depressed and simply have a new look or a new tool to hang in their garage.

Eventually, we get tired of the self-pity and decide that some change is probably better than none, so we start looking for quick fixes and instant relief. We try a new diet, dump our thoughtless friends or abusive spouses, sign up for that community education class we always wanted to take, and buy more stuff, all in the hope that something will change the color of life and miraculously banish our depression. We may try to be somebody different by moving to another location and taking on a new job. At one point, I moved from Minnesota to Mississippi to accept a church secretary job. Talk about a drastic change! Did it help? Nope.

My Story

God has given each of us a framework within which to live our lives. He has deliberately placed each of us in a particular family group, in a particular location, and in a particular school or church or workplace to provide us with our human connections. He's given each of us specific desires, talents, and skills to provide direction and purpose for our lives. Within that specific framework, He is working to transform who we are now into the beautiful person He's already created us to be.

God's particular framework for my life is music. I grew up in a musical family. Mom was the church organist for over fifty years and has a lovely soprano voice. Dad sang with a men's quartet for many years. My older brother sang and played the trumpet, my two younger brothers are professional bass guitarists, and my sister is an accomplished piano accompanist in an Iowa public school.

I learned at a young age that I felt right at home at the piano. I began taking piano lessons from Mom when I was six years old. By the time I was twelve, I had become comfortable playing the piano at church for various youth group activities. Music is in my genes! My musical family surrounded and suffused my very being with music. Although I was aware from a young age that my musical talent had come from God, it wouldn't occur to me until much later in my life that He had a special purpose for that talent and passion other than "making joyful noise to the Lord." Why would it occur to me? I was just a kid who loved to play the piano!

My passion for the piano was increasingly important to me as I became a teenager and entered what would be a lifelong struggle with depression. I didn't like that shy girl in the mirror: a stubborn, withdrawn individual whose only redeeming value seemed to be her musical ability. Eventually I began to learn that being a good piano player brought me the attention I longed for, and the designation of piano accompanist soon became my identity. I wrapped the piano around me like a security blanket and basked in the attention and approval of friends who lavished praise and admiration upon me. I became addicted to the piano because all of that attention filled some dark, empty place inside me. I retreated to my hiding place at the piano to camouflage the depth of my pain. I was so attached to the piano that I felt naked and vulnerable without it. I used the piano throughout my life to isolate myself from people and keep my secret safe: *I'm just a plain, boring, unlovable individual whose only value is to keep my mouth shut and tickle the ivories.*

That belief played havoc with my ability to establish and maintain healthy relationships. Over the years, many friends walked away, probably because I seemed a lot like Charlie Brown's friend Pigpen, except instead of a cloud of dirt, I had dark clouds of gloom surrounding me. My perception of myself as flawed and unworthy remained unchanged, and I continued to sense an oppressive undercurrent of "not-okay-ness."

Once I graduated from college with a music degree and had to face the music, figure out who I was, and discover what possible role I could fill in this world, it didn't take long to lose what little confidence I had. Fortunately (or more likely, by God's grace and perfect planning), my skill at the keyboard kept me from totally giving up on life. Although I ultimately earned my living in the business world, making music as a piano accompanist consistently brought me great comfort and joy.

God continued to open up various opportunities for me to play for small groups, church choirs, and soloists. For twenty amazing years, through my forties and into my early sixties, I had the privilege and sweet pleasure of being the choir accompanist at one of the megachurches in the Minneapolis area. The opportunity to play regularly with a fifty-piece orchestra and a 120-voice choir greatly improved my piano skills. Added to that cherished privilege was the unexpected delight of working with the church's drama team. We rehearsed and performed dinner theater musicals annually. With that group of actors and musicians, my knowledge of music was challenged well beyond anything I had dreamed of as a child. I never imagined I would be awake in the wee hours of many nights, practicing difficult show tunes as well as transposing and rewriting the music to fit our small cast of actors and singers.

Because I'd become a people pleaser and a yes girl, I continued to play the piano while trying to hide my horrible deformity called depression. Although I still found familiarity and comfort in the act of playing the piano and creating music, eventually there was no longer any joy in my playing. I was simply going through the motions; playing the piano became a noose around my neck. I began to resent the ever-growing demands on my time and energies, but I didn't dare say no to the many opportunities to play for fear of losing the attention and approval of my friends and the church leaders.

As my depression deepened and I became needier and clingier with certain friends, my passion for the piano became stained with the beginnings of bitterness and a growing rage I didn't understand. My emotional feet got stuck in the muck, and I felt abandoned and alone as some of my friends gradually began to distance themselves from me—or perhaps it was I who distanced myself from them.

Causes of Depression

Depression has been researched extensively for years, and much has been learned about the biology of depression. Some depression can be influenced by medical conditions such as hypothyroidism, hypoglycemia, glandular functions, seasonal affective disorder (SAD), fibromyalgia, rheumatoid arthritis, and menopause and postpartum blues in women. However, scientists' understanding and discoveries are far from complete.

It isn't the purpose of this book to define the specific symptoms of depression or the wide range of therapies available, but I want to focus briefly on two issues that I believe are important: medication and diet.

Medication

Because depression can be caused by body chemistry that we aren't even aware of, it's extremely important to seek out a medical doctor to find out if there is a medical issue or a chemical deficiency that could benefit from medication.

Serotonin is the primary chemical that affects mood. The more serotonin in the brain, the higher a person's mood. If the level of serotonin drops, depression may occur. That's why many of the drugs available to treat depression have an effect on one's serotonin level. Serotonin is believed to help regulate mood, social behavior, appetite, digestion, sexual desire, sleep, and memory. Serotonin can make it easier for the brain to function more efficiently, enabling the settling of the person's moods and more rational thinking.

Not all drugs containing serotonin react the same way in everybody. Based on my own experience with medication, I caution you not to view any antidepressant drug as a perfect solution. We tend to think that if we just take a pill every day, everything will be all right. But even the best of medications designed specifically for depression can't resolve all of the problems. I've been taking generic Prozac (fluoxetine) for years but still sink into dark days of depression from time to time. The drug has certainly been helpful, but it hasn't been a cure-all.

There have been many times over the years when I wanted to stop taking the drug because I was feeling good and thought I could manage life without it. I did try stopping once or twice without my doctor's permission, and I regretted it. The important thing I learned was that my body wasn't able to keep its serotonin levels stable without the help of the drug. It's similar to being a diabetic: the body needs insulin, and because diabetics' bodies are unable to keep the levels of insulin stable, they must take insulin for the rest of their lives. I hated the idea that I would have to be on a drug for the rest of my life just to feel good. Unfortunately, our bodies aren't perfect, so we need the help of science to keep everything in good working order.

Diet

It has been shown that healthier diets can be helpful in combating depression. The National Center for Biotechnology Information (NCBI) investigated the most nutrient-dense sources that play a role in the prevention of and recovery from depressive disorders. In an article by Laura R. LaChance and Drew Ramsey in the September 2018 issue of World Journal of Psychiatry,[1] these twelve antidepressant nutrients were specifically listed.

- folate
- iron
- long-chain omega-3 fatty acids (EPA and DHA)
- magnesium
- potassium
- selenium
- thiamine
- vitamin A
- vitamin B6
- vitamin B12
- vitamin C
- zinc

The writers indicated that deficiencies of certain nutrients can cause depressive symptoms.

> Studies have found that "traditional" or "whole foods" dietary patterns are significantly correlated with a decrease of depressive disorders or symptoms … Common recommendations were to increase the consumption of fruit, vegetables, fiber, and fish.

Life Is Confusing

There are probably as many reasons for depression as there are people. Multiple researchers have agreed that a vast number of mental health issues like depression and anxiety are a direct result of our self-defeating thinking or our desperate reactions to the stressors that clutter up and disrupt our daily lives. The common problems that interrupt our lives are much the same for all of us simply because we weren't taught things like how to set boundaries, how to get in touch with our feelings, how to make better choices, or how to think about what we think about. We may have learned some of these lessons in the school of hard knocks, but we often learned them incorrectly because either we were listening to the wrong voices or we weren't hearing and applying the truth.

As a piano player, I can easily compare dealing with the intricacies and frustrations of doing life with learning to play the piano. It would be too difficult for a beginning piano student to combine all of the unique aspects of learning a page of music all at once, so a good teacher starts with the simple ABCs and saves teaching the more difficult aspects of music, like an insane key signature or an unusually funky rhythm, for later.

When I'm practicing a piece of music on the piano, I don't like it when people are watching me. They expect to hear the whole piece played flawlessly; but I need to practice! The whole purpose of practicing is to identify the problems that need fixing in order to avoid stumbling during the actual performance. As soon as I encounter a mistake or a difficult passage, I stop and break it down into manageable parts to see what is causing the problem.

- It could be a tricky rhythm that I need to count out carefully and play several times, one hand at a time, to understand and feel how both hands must work together.
- It could be a particular chord that stretches my short fingers too far. I may need to revise the chord so it fits my hand better without diminishing the overall structure and sound.
- It could be an awkward page turn that needs work. Yes, musicians even need to practice turning the pages. Suddenly stopping the music to fumble with a page turn is not cool!

Small Steps Suffice

You don't need to know why there is a problem as you learn new ways of doing life as an adult. You do need to be able to identify the problem before you can fix it.

When we're depressed, we tend to work hard at looking nice and acting normal. We believe that's what people want and expect of us: no mistakes, no hysterics. Whether in musical performance or in life, it can be frightening to enter a new and strange situation where we're expected to perform like mature, experienced human beings with no mistakes. That's why we need to start with the ABCs of life and practice one or two aspects of our daily difficulties at a time.

- Are you afraid of meeting new people or taking on a new job, fearing that you might not live up to the expectations of others?
- Are you struggling with financial difficulties because of an addiction to shopping or drugs, or because you're facing an expensive purchase for your house or an unexpected medical procedure?
- Are you distressed or angry about giving up your limited time and energy to another person who is manipulative and needy?
- Are you feeling inadequate or discouraged because your out-of-control teenager or elderly parent is demanding more time and energy than your weary mind and hectic schedule can handle?

Each day of your life is a practice session as you learn how to get through one day and move on to the next without losing hope. It's better to take small steps into new behaviors and attitudes. You don't have to conquer every problem and arrive at your destination today! Focusing on one issue at a time will enable you to strengthen your thinking and responses in that particular area before trying to move on to another more difficult issue. An old story about a donkey illustrates what I mean.

> One day a farmer's donkey fell down into a well. The animal cried piteously for hours as the farmer tried to figure out how to get the donkey out. Finally, he decided it was impossible and, because the animal was old and the well was dry anyway, it just wasn't worth it to try and retrieve the donkey. The farmer asked his neighbors to come over and help him cover up the well. They all grabbed shovels and began to shovel dirt into the well.
>
> At first, when the donkey realized what was happening, he became frightened and cried horribly. Then surprisingly, he quieted down and let out some happy brays. Several shovelfuls later, the farmer looked into the well to see what was happening and was astonished at what he saw. With every shovelful of dirt that was tossed into the well, the donkey was shaking it off and taking a step up. As the farmer's neighbors continued to shovel dirt on top of the animal, he continued to shake it off and take another step up. Pretty

soon, to everyone's amazement, the donkey stepped up over the edge of the well and trotted off!

—author unknown[2]

I love that story!

Just like that donkey, when you're depressed, you feel helpless, like you're being buried alive. However, what happens to you isn't nearly as important as how you respond to it. By figuring out the smallest step you can take, you can begin to make deliberate new choices and learn new ways of thinking and behaving. You can begin to exert some control over those outside forces that drag you down, and you can learn the necessary skills to more successfully operate in your world.

Don't put pressure on yourself to quickly understand and resolve a problem that may have taken months or years to develop. Learning how to live with or in spite of depression requires time and practice, persistence and courage. Be patient with the process and be gentle with yourself along the way.

Look Up and Step Out

Do you recognize the framework God is using to build your confidence and teach you the life lessons He wants you to know? No matter who you are or how you make a living—schoolteacher, mom, truck driver, doctor, secretary, construction worker, pastor, janitor, tennis pro— God has intentionally placed you in a specific family, town, vocation, and church community. He is intent on using your experiences, your relationships, and even your depression and failures to show you who He is and how much He loves you. His greatest desire is that you grow in your knowledge of Him as you mature in your ability to do life as a child of the King.

Even if you feel like the whole world is shoveling dirt into that hole you're buried in, you can receive hope and encouragement from the Lord, and you can hold tightly to His hand as you begin to shake off the dirt and take a step up. As you contemplate the common questions with which life confronts you, Jesus will guide you through the necessary pain, dry your tears, and show you the way to conquer your fear, banish those unwelcome thoughts, and reconcile those awkward relationships.

The apostle Paul declares this in Romans 5:3–5 (NCV).

We have joy with our troubles, because we know that these troubles produce patience. And patience produces character, and character produces hope. And this hope will never disappoint us, because God has poured out his love to fill our hearts.

Even though God may allow our lives to include depression and anxiety, He will use those personal struggles to teach us important life lessons and to draw us into a closer relationship with Himself. And He will always tell the Truth.

As you walk with Him:

- He can show you how to discern which habits or choices may be hindering your growth.
- He can show you what attitudes or behaviors need to be corrected to interact in a healthy way with the important people in your life.
- He can show you new ways of thinking about yourself and about life.
- He can teach you to quietly trust Him while you wait for His next instructions.

God has made this promise to everyone who comes to Him.

So do not fear, for I am with you; do not be dismayed, for I am your God. I will strengthen you and help you; I will uphold you with my righteous right hand. All who rage against you will surely be ashamed and disgraced; those who oppose you will be as nothing and perish. Though you search for your enemies, you will not find them. Those who wage war against you will be as nothing at all. For I am the Lord your God who takes hold of your right hand and says to you, Do not fear; I will help you. (Isaiah 41:10–13)

When you start asking better questions about how to do life and building your life on the foundation of God's Truth, things will change! Jesus can literally transform your thinking and rewrite your story when you are open to His grace and willing to trust His guidance.

Chapter 2
Who Do You Think You Are?

You may have heard this question from a parent or teacher who thought you were getting a bit too big for your britches, from the school bully who was trying to belittle you, or from your boss who thought you had overstepped your authority.

For sixteen years, I worked for a small company where employees were told we were valuable members of the team with important contributions to make to the overall success of the business. That made me feel good because I was finally being told in direct ways that I had some good ideas that were worth listening to and possibly implementing. After several years, I had become quite efficient at my particular job. I had been able to streamline a number of my department's weekly processes to the point where the company was able to eliminate a couple of the positions that had been needed to complete the various tasks on time each week.

Then one year, the CEO and managers had the not-so-brilliant idea to bring us together in a series of so-called team-building meetings. Throughout the duration of this yearlong experiment, we were all asked to contribute our ideas about ways to improve the inner workings of the company, within our own departments as well as throughout the company as a team.

I began to express some of my own ideas about more efficient processes and better communication. Much to my chagrin, those build-me-up kudos about my good ideas soon turned into put-downs. The powers that be clearly weren't expecting me to be so bold in offering suggestions! One email response from the CEO was, in my opinion, quite harsh: *You have no business trying to be a manager. You're out of your league.*

It was evident that my suggestions had been badly misinterpreted! I had no desire to be a manager. I was simply offering suggestions based on my own experiences with the company's various processes. I actually cried when I read that email. The CEO might as well have run me through a shredder. Ultimately, it came as no surprise that the result of a year's worth of seminars and weekly meetings was a precipitous drop in morale throughout the company and the end of any meaningful or timely communication among the members of this now-broken team.

As you might imagine, I stopped offering suggestions. Extreme reaction? Probably. I also stopped trusting the CEO and his managers to treat me with respect as a valued member of the team. I didn't know how else to respond because those harsh words cut right to the core of my own judgment about myself: *I can't do anything right. I'm worthless.*

You may have been in situations like this where one day you were being built up and encouraged to be the best you can be, and the next day you were kicked in the head and crushed with comments or actions that suggested you were already the best you could be—and that wasn't much!

If you hear words like this often enough throughout your life, spoken in anger or in ignorance, you eventually develop an overly cynical way of looking at yourself.

- Do you constantly berate and undervalue yourself? "I'm such a klutz." "I'm so stupid."
- What are the main messages you hear in your head about who you are and about your own worth? Are they encouraging or judgmental? Pleasant or bitter?

Similar but Unique

God has created every individual on this planet to be unique. We certainly are that, in more ways than one! It's true that we're born with similar characteristics. We have physical bodies, and we're either male or female (at least according to our Maker's design). We were each given the ability to feel a whole array of emotions, ranging from happy to sad, from upbeat to downcast, from enthusiastic to world-weary. We have intricately formed brains that control our bodies' vast range of motions, reflexes, internal processes, and senses. We have minds with which to think, to create and imagine, to feel deeply, and to be unique individuals.

That's where the similarities end! We come in all shapes and sizes, with all types of personalities, different facial features, different hair colors (some of our own choosing), different ancestors, different interests, and more. There's no one else on earth exactly like you. You may sound just like your grandfather, but you're not your grandfather. You may look just like your mother, but you're not your mother. (I can hear some of you saying, "Thank goodness!")

I used to watch a fascinating television show called *Who Do You Think You Are?* This show was a venue through which various celebrities explored their family histories and learned some surprising and enlightening things about their ancestors' lives and beliefs. What intrigued me was that most of those celebrities were able to identify certain characteristics such as determination, unselfishness, adaptability, courage, or competitiveness that seemed to be passed on through the family gene pool. Some also found other not-so-favorable traits like dishonesty, stubbornness, greediness, and prejudice. I don't know much about my Scottish and English ancestors, but I suspect that my stubborn independence came from someone in my family line. At least, that's my excuse!

Even though doing genealogical research can be fun and educational, most of us don't have the interest, resources, or time to pursue that endeavor. If you do have an interest, there are numerous resources available, including these online sites.

- Ancestry.com
- 23 & Me (DNA genetic testing)
- myheritage.com
- familysearch.org

You don't really need to know who your ancestors were to begin understanding who you are. Besides, many of you would likely find more rascals and rags than royalty and riches in your ancestral closets. Although I can brag about being a distant relative of Mary, Queen of Scots, I don't shout that news too boldly because that particular queen was commonly known as Bloody Mary. I wonder which character trait I got from her!

Because of the pressures of society and the various difficulties you encounter in your journey through life, you may have either lost or forfeited your ability to be who you really are. Instead, you try to become what everyone else expects you to be. You try to look like everyone else; you try to sound like everyone else; you try to act like everyone else; you try to please everyone else. You ultimately become even more uncomfortable, confused, and depressed because the fact is no matter how hard you try, you can't be like everybody else. You're not meant to be like everybody else! Our imaginative Creator made you to be you and nobody else.

What Do You Believe about Life?

Has anyone ever asked you to share something personal about yourself? What did you say? I'm guessing you would first mention the kind of work you're currently engaged in, your single or married status, and your family. You might mention the town where you grew up, your college education or lack of it, and possibly some aspects of your personality that are easily noticeable, like your sense of humor or your shyness.

There are certain things you can't change, like how or where you were raised, your memories of people and past events, and your initial interpretation of those events. There are other things that can have a significant impact on who you have become, like what you were taught to believe about life. People do what they do and think what they think because of what they believe. Beliefs are the primary source of our attitudes, responses, feelings, and actions. Every time you look in the mirror, you see what you believe. You believe that you're too tall, you're too fat, your hair is too thin or too curly, or your nose is too prominent. You get the idea. Those things can set you up with self-defacing and self-destructive beliefs and behaviors that can imprison you in the fog of depression.

Where do those beliefs come from? Your parents and other important adults served as mirrors for you. The things they did and said—about themselves, about you, and about the world—became the beliefs, values, biases, and opinions you adopted as the truth for your own life. You also learned through books, radio, television, the internet, schoolteachers, church leaders, and neighbors.

We all come from different backgrounds, and these backgrounds have determined who we are, what we believe, how we think, and how we respond to any given situation. Who you are right now is a direct result of the messages you received as a child from your family and society and incorporated into your own belief system. A farmer from Iowa will view life differently than a wealthy businessman from New York. A girl whose father was a beloved pastor will have different values than a girl whose father was alcoholic and abusive.

It's generally agreed by many researchers that children have a pretty solid idea by age six what they believe to be right and wrong, fair and unfair, good and bad. Children typically view themselves as the center of their universe, so their perception is that everything that happens revolves around, is caused by, or is directed toward them. You've probably heard comments like these "Momilies."[3]

- If you can't say anything nice, don't say anything at all.
- You've got a face only a mother could love.
- Try to pretend you're normal.
- Children are meant to be seen and not heard.
- Is that the best you could do?
- Look at me when I'm talking to you.
- Good boys don't cry.

Depending on how you worked out those childhood beliefs in your daily activities and relationships, your perspectives may have become totally irrational and dysfunctional as you started to filter your entire adult experience through the beliefs of a six-year-old child. Additionally, every distorted thought you have about yourself triggers a matching distortion about others.

- If you believe you are bad and deserve to be punished, you will see others as judgmental and harsh.
- If you believe you don't matter, you will see others as neglectful and dismissing.
- If you were regularly reprimanded or criticized, you believe you must always strive to be perfect and will see others as impossible to please.
- If you were physically or emotionally neglected or not provided with adequate attention and care, you will believe that no one will provide caring support—you're on your own in the world.

- If you were abused or shamed in any way, you will believe you're unimportant and powerless and will see others as unsympathetic and not to be trusted.
- If you received approval, encouragement, and buckets of loving attention, you will see others as giving and approachable.

Core Beliefs

If you want to know what your true beliefs are, look at the things you do and the way you treat yourself, others, and everything around you. Your core beliefs dictate

- what you think of yourself,
- what you are and are not allowed to do and be,
- how you are to behave and react to people and experiences, and
- what you can and cannot expect.

You rarely question the validity of your own beliefs. Why would you? That would be too much like labeling yourself as faulty. Once you believe something is the way it should be, you follow that path strictly, as if you're being dragged along by some mysterious force that ominously whispers, "Resistance is futile."

Irrational beliefs cause you to have rigid expectations of yourself and others, which you claim as absolutes. Here are some common examples.

- I don't deserve to get what I want or need.
- I must do everything perfectly, or I am incompetent.
- I must have everybody's approval before I make a decision.
- Saying no to a request is always a selfish thing to do.
- My worth depends on my achievements.
- I should always feel and appear happy, confident, and in control of myself.

No one is perfect! We all come with baggage. Even the apostle Paul admitted that he struggled with his own stuff when he said, "I do not understand the things I do. I do not do what I want to do, and I do the things I hate. What a miserable man I am!" (Romans 7:15 NCV). Yet he goes on to say "Who will save me from this body that brings me death?

I thank God for saving me through Jesus Christ our Lord!" (Romans 7:24–25 NCV).

We unconsciously buy into what others have told us about ourselves and the world around us. What if you could challenge and change your belief system? Good news: you can! Although your past has shaped today's perceptions, beliefs, and behaviors, the past is history. You can certainly learn from it, but you don't have to be controlled by it. If you're living out a certain belief just because that's what you've always been told, it's time to challenge that belief. Stop and ask yourself why you believe a particular teaching is true, appropriate, or even rational.

With practice, you can move away from that preprogrammed person who keeps thinking the worst and doing what you don't want to do into a person who actually reflects the independent, more confident you. When you follow the advice of your Creator and Lord, Jesus Christ, and listen to what He says about who you are in His eyes, feeling more secure is a guarantee. You will learn that He has made you, not to be perfect in the eyes of the world but perfect in His eyes. The apostle Paul speaks these words to you in 2 Corinthians 12:9–10.

> But he said to me, "My grace is sufficient for you, for my power is made perfect in weakness." Therefore I will boast all the more gladly about my weaknesses, so that Christ's power may rest on me. That is why, for Christ's sake, I delight in weaknesses, in insults, in hardships, in persecutions, in difficulties. For when I am weak, then I am strong.

Is It Really You?

Your personality tends to be the one thing about you that everyone in your world sees and interacts with. If you've taken any of the numerous personality inventories available, you've probably discovered that there are several basic personality types, and there are multiple ways of sorting them out. Everyone has the general characteristics and tendencies of more than one personality type but will lean toward one or two. The patterns you find in these various personality assessments tend to remain stable throughout your life and accurately portray your overall outlook on and approach to life.

The important thing to remember is that there is no good or bad personality type. They were all created by God!

There are various ways of describing or categorizing personalities. The familiar Myers-Briggs[4] personality inventory sets out four basic personality types.

- Introversion vs. Extroversion
- Intuition vs. Sensing
- Thinking vs. Feeling
- Judging vs. Perceiving

These categories are then broken out into sixteen more specific categories.

Another inventory identifies personality types in four basic categories or temperaments:[5] Popular Sanguine ("Let's do it the *fun* way"), Powerful Choleric ("Let's do it *my* way"), Perfect Melancholy ("Let's do it the *right* way"), and Peaceful Phlegmatic ("Let's do it the *easy* way").

A different sort of inventory can be found in the book *Freeing Your Mind from Memories That Bind*.[6] I especially enjoyed this inventory because it highlighted my strengths and didn't make my weaknesses sound so horrible!

Your personality is displayed in the actions you take and the decisions you make. Generally, people will act the same in a variety of situations because of their specific personality traits: either you are a patient person or not, a responsible person or not, an organized person or not. These ingrained traits will likely remain the same throughout your life. However, in many cases you do have some control over certain aspects of your personality.

- You can learn to become more patient
- You can learn to become more responsible
- You can learn to become more organized
- You can learn to be more cooperative
- You can learn to be less aggressive and controlling
- You can learn to be less angry and sarcastic
- You can learn to be less anxious and fearful

You can focus your efforts on those things about yourself that you can either change or adapt to your particular situation. Instead of asking, "Why am I like that?" start asking, "Since I am like that, how can I make that characteristic work for me instead of against me?"

For an example, let's look at one of the more common differences in personalities: extroverts* and introverts.

Extroverts/Introverts

These are traits that you can't really change about your personality. However, it is possible to change some behaviors associated with these traits.

I struggled for years with my introversion because I felt different somehow from the people around me. My friends always enjoyed being together in groups, but I would rather be with my best friend or alone with my thoughts, my books, and my music. I didn't seem to fit with other people, and I began to believe this indicated some kind of character flaw. I felt ashamed and out of place.

It was only years later that I finally became aware of the distinction between introverts and extroverts and was able to scrape off one thick layer of muck that was contributing to my depression.

We tend to view being extroverted or introverted as an either/or characteristic.

- An extrovert is energized by being with people; an introvert becomes exhausted around people, especially in a particularly loud or exuberant crowd. The crowds at the Minnesota State Fair have that effect on me! I eventually reach a breaking point when I have to find a quiet and separate space to be alone and recharge my emotional batteries.
- An extrovert is delighted to welcome all of his friends into his home, almost at any time; an introvert's home is a place to get away from people. I have to think long and hard before inviting anyone into my private "girl cave."

---

* For you spelling purists, the original spelling for extrovert was *extra*vert, with *extra* meaning outside and *intro* meaning inside. However, *extro*vert is an acceptable and more popular way to spell it. Because I'm independent, stubborn, and eager to be popular, I'm spelling it with an *o*.

- An extrovert doesn't particularly enjoy being alone and seeks out friends who fulfill his need for regular companionship; an introvert especially appreciates friends who understand and accommodate her occasional need to be alone.

There are more extroverts in the world than introverts. Our society tends to cater to the extroverts who tend to be "out there," sometimes intruding themselves into private parties. On the flip side, introverts are neither seen nor heard unless they want to be!

Most people can comfortably alternate between the two extremes. Even though I'm comfortable being alone, I also enjoy being with people, especially those who are deep thinkers like I am and who make me laugh. Through trial and error, I've learned that if I'm around people for too long, even people I like and enjoy, my mind and emotions begin to shut down, my eyes glaze over, and I mentally drift away into that quiet place inside my head.

Most of the people I hang out with are extroverts who have a hard time understanding where I've gone when my mind drifts away to recharge, so I've made some adjustments to accommodate those difficulties.

- I've learned that it is my responsibility to let people know when I need or want to be socially available. I used to get upset and sad whenever it seemed that no one was paying attention to me. I wasn't aware that my introverted behavior had drawn a curtain around me and blocked anyone from coming too close. I've had to teach people that my curtain of privacy is not an impenetrable wall.
- I've learned to be more selective about the situations and events in which I choose to participate. I've turned down invitations to certain public events knowing that being in a loud, crowded venue can set off alarm bells in my nervous system.
- In situations when I'm forced to be with people for an extended period of time, like a two-day work seminar where I was with coworkers for eight to ten hours both days, I've learned how to make an occasional graceful exit so I can take a quiet break and escape the human noise.

There have been other times when I've deliberately donned my extrovert hat and forced myself to be outgoing in a situation that felt scary or uncomfortable. After moving from a megachurch where I'd been a well-established piano accompanist for twenty years and was acquainted with hundreds of people, to a smaller church where I had no particular role and only a few new acquaintances, I needed to cultivate new relationships. I pretended to be an extrovert so I could behave like one. This process was quite exhausting yet productive. My self-confidence grew, and my general attitude around people I didn't know gradually became more open and available. The delightful result of that nerve-wracking process is that I now have numerous friends who used to be just names and faces. I admit, though, when I've had more than enough of the extroverted "people-izing," it's always a relief to go home to my girl cave and listen to the soothing sounds of silence.

What Are You Good At?

We each have some talent or skill that we've been drawn to and have developed over time, which brings great satisfaction and a sense of purpose.

- A talent is an innate, inborn ability, something you're naturally good at and are drawn to.
- A skill is something you've worked to perfect, either because of a personal interest or because of a work requirement.

A skill can be learned by anyone who has the capacity, potential, and willingness to learn. Even if you don't have a particular talent, you can still apply yourself to learning the necessary skill to, for example, play a musical instrument or grow a beautiful garden.

Although I enjoy looking at plants and flowers and greatly respect people who are able to create beautiful gardens and flower arrangements, this is definitely not one of my talents or skills. I learned long ago that green things die in my presence! However, I do have an innate talent for music, having grown up surrounded by musicians. As a result, I devoted myself to acquiring the necessary skills to play the piano well, specifically as an accompanist. I chose the role of accompanist rather than soloist because it has brought me the most challenge and pleasure—and because I'm an introvert, and solos scare me!

You usually know what skills are needed to perform in a particular job, like managing finances or working with machinery. But is that where your true interests and talents lie? Is your work stimulating and creative, or are you daydreaming of doing something else that appeals more to your interest in photography or art or growing green things?

Sometimes the talent you're most passionate about doesn't meet the high skill level required to pursue a successful career, like my little girl dream of being a concert pianist. You then choose a job that you may not be particularly interested in simply because you need the paycheck. There's nothing wrong with that. You may simply need to look outside the workplace to find activities that bring you pleasure and a sense of accomplishment and reward.

A skill or talent that is currently only a hobby can often be turned into a volunteer opportunity, such as assisting a family with home repairs or offering piano lessons to a needy family. Your skill could also morph into an entrepreneurial enterprise that becomes a booming business.

A book called *Now, Discover Your Strengths*[7] by Marcus Buckingham and Donald O. Clifton can be a valuable resource if you wish to learn about and evaluate your own skills and abilities. There is also a companion book called *StrengthsFinder 2.0*[8] by Tom Rath, which includes a StrengthsFinder Profile that has assisted and motivated many people to turn their talents into strengths.

It's always helpful to find out what your strengths are, not only in terms of your personality but also in terms of your life skills. God has given you those particular desires, interests, and talents to continually draw you to a place where you feel fulfilled, and He is able to use those interests and talents to encourage and uplift you during those times when you're stuck in depression and feeling unsatisfied or uncomfortable with yourself.

Do You Remember ...?

Each individual is unique. We've lived unique lives in unique families and in unique settings. As a result, our memories are highly unique. Some memories, whether pleasant or unpleasant, seem just as fresh today as when the events actually happened. We can be transported back to another time and another place by sounds, smells, songs, holidays, and images. We've all had those déjà vu experiences.

Whenever I smell cigar smoke, I drift back to my childhood when my Grandpa Bever was actively farming. I enjoyed standing in the storm cellar and watching him clean and box up eggs for market as he puffed on his cigar. I dearly loved him, and it was obvious that he enjoyed my presence there with him. I treasure those precious memories.

Most of our memories are harmless and have no significant impact on our emotional well-being. Sadly, some people carry painful memories with them every day. No matter how hard they try to forget, the events are as fresh as when they first happened and continue to upset them for years.

Other people spend their emotional energy on digging expeditions, trying to unearth portions of their childhood they can't remember, believing this may free them from some horrible childhood trauma.

I was determined to explore every nook and cranny of my life because I was sure I would discover some awful event that had damaged me and caused my depression. I was certain that once I uncovered that imagined horror, I could fix it or at least come to grips with it, thereby escaping my prison of depression. Then one night I had a strange vision.

I was standing beside Jesus at the entrance to a large, untended garden that appeared to be laid out like a giant maze. There were dark, confusing tunnels that led through tall, tangled grasses and thick thorns.

As I stood at the edge of that dreary place, Jesus assured me that I didn't have to go through that confusing, hazardous maze to find what I was searching for. He claimed He could quickly and easily take me around to the other side and explain to me what I wanted to know so I could avoid getting tangled up and injured.

I stubbornly stood my ground and told Jesus I had to go through the maze. Even though He knew He had a better way to answer my gnawing questions about my pain and bitterness, He smiled as He took my hand and said, "If that's what you think you need to do, I'll stay beside you all the way."

Stubborn girl! Why must I always learn my lessons the hard way? If I had only let Jesus lead me, my search for answers may have taken much less time and effort. But I had to run out ahead of Him and go my own way. Did I find what I hoped to? Nope, not in that maze! Was all of that fearful, painful searching worth it? Well, sort of. I did confirm that what

I was looking for wasn't there, and I learned an important lesson about running ahead of Jesus: don't do it!

I'm not saying that going on a search through your past is a bad thing. However, I believe that if God wants to reveal something from your past that will enlighten and motivate you to make needed changes in what you believe about yourself, He will allow you to recall it—but only when He knows you're ready to hear the Truth. He's well aware of how a long-forgotten event may have confused or hurt you and deeply affected your life. He knows exactly what it will take for you to overcome or resolve any damage caused by that situation. He also knows the best time in your emotional and spiritual growth to begin the healing process.

Jesus waited more than forty years to uncover a painful memory from my childhood that had been lost and buried.

Grandpa, Part 1: Trauma

My Grandpa Bever suffered a debilitating stroke and became bedridden when I was only eleven years old. Grandma took care of him at home for well over a year. The only thing I remember clearly about that time was that Grandma had to put him in a wheelchair and wheel him out to the dining room to feed him. That holiday season, as I watched Grandpa being wheeled past me, I stared at him because he didn't look like the Grandpa I knew and loved. His hair was askew, he was thin and pale, his toenails had grown long, and he didn't smell very good. I didn't know how to think or act as I tried to understand what I was seeing. Then, in one awful moment, time stopped for me and everything changed. Grandpa turned his head, looked right at me, and immediately started to cry. In that instant, something in my little girl heart broke. I thought I had upset him by staring at him. When Grandpa died some months later, I knew in my already broken heart that it was my fault he'd gone away.

The first part of any memory involves the historical facts that can't be changed. That day was the last time I saw Grandpa before he died. Nothing will ever change that. It happened, and there's nothing I can do about it.

The second part of a memory involves the feelings generated by the memory. At the time of that event, I felt sad and deeply confused by Grandpa's appearance and disability, and I felt devastated in the moment when he looked at me and started to cry.

The third part of the memory is the irrational belief that becomes entangled with and eventually redefines the event and its associated feelings. Because I wasn't aware of certain circumstances in my family in the years just before and after Grandpa's death, I believed I wasn't getting much attention from my parents. Given that I never heard them mention Grandpa again after his death, I was further convinced that they blamed me for his absence.

I was too young and immature to understand that the heavy weight of that significant death of my mom's father, as well as the demands of five young children (including the delicate and critical health of my baby sister), were pulling my parents in too many directions emotionally. I believe now that my parents likely decided that I and my older brother, then twelve and thirteen years old, respectively, could take care of ourselves through those months of emotional and physical distress. At the time, however, I was as convinced as any young child could be that I'd done something really bad. I was unable to process all that was going on emotionally in my family, and I concluded that Grandpa's death was my fault and my parents no longer loved me.

Because memories don't stay fresh in our minds, our interpretation of the actual event can become distorted over time and take on a life of its own. Even though my memory was buried in the past, the wound remained, and over the years I began to build habits of behavior and thinking to protect myself from the painful feelings and hidden beliefs associated with feeling at fault and unloved. Those beliefs and habits of behavior caused my view of myself to become significantly distorted and pessimistic. Over time I became clingier and more manipulative with certain friends as I tried to compensate for the perceived lack of affection and attention at home. This clingy behavior caused some people to turn away from me, further confirming my belief that I was no longer lovable or even necessary. I assumed that everyone I loved would abandon me, and my depression deepened.

When a past event in your life such as a confusing childhood experience or trauma has been misinterpreted and buried, that part of yourself isn't able to grow and develop as you move into adulthood. I became emotionally stuck at age twelve, and I remained there for years.

The things from your past that have influenced your beliefs about yourself and your world have taken years to develop into the behaviors and beliefs you have now. You can be easily shocked and appalled when you suddenly erupt into a fit of anger or spout bitter, irrational accusations. You think, *Where did that come from?* My outbursts came from the confusion, fear, and resentment of a twelve-year-old who believed she had been abandoned to fend for herself for the rest of her miserable life.

Today Never Comes

Life consists in a procession of yesterdays and tomorrows.
I've often wished to discover the joy of just one today ...
but today never comes.

My days are spent in the memories of my yesterdays:
days of laughter, music, pain, and tears,
and of yesterday's dreams that never became realities.

I dream of a life of contentment,
of knowing who I am and where I belong.
But today comes only for those who can live at peace
with the yesterdays that still haunt them.

For me, today never comes
because today is only yesterday's dream
and tomorrow's memory.

You live only in the present; you can't change the past. Thankfully, God can teach you the truth about your past and begin to develop in you more accurate and more mature beliefs about who you are as an adult in the present.

You can't go back and change the beginning, but you can
start where you are and change the ending.
—C. S. Lewis[9]

What Do You Think of Yourself?

What you think of yourself matters a great deal! You are not just your name or your gender. You are not just your personality or your behavior. You are not just your skills or your memories. You're a complicated mixture of many parts, and trying to figure out who you are is a bit like trying to learn a new song.

Any musician who looks at a piece of music for the first time sees a page cluttered with black splotches of different shapes and sizes. There are straight lines, jagged and curvy symbols, numbers, foreign words, and many black and white circles. Depending on the difficulty of the piece, it can take significant time and effort to make the cluttered page sound the way the composer intended.

Similarly, when you're depressed, all you see in yourself is a jumbled package of old, dark stuff that has defined and changed your psyche. Your fractured mind seems to play against you, leaving you in total confusion as you try to figure out what's wrong.

Do you see yourself as permanently flawed and hopelessly unable to change? Do you believe you're unlovable and unwanted?

I can promise you it wasn't Jesus who told you that!

Take Jesus at His word! Start seeing yourself as He sees you and hearing the song of life He's composed just for you.

- **You are His child.** "How great is the love the Father has lavished on us, that we should be called children of God! And that is what we are! The reason the world does not know us is that it did not know him." (1 John 3:1)
- **You are secure in His love.** "For I am convinced that neither death, nor life, neither angels nor demons, neither the present nor the future, nor any powers, neither height nor depth, nor anything else in all creation, will be able to separate us from the love of God that is in Christ Jesus our Lord." (Romans 8:38–39)
- **You are strong and can do anything with His help.** "I can do everything through him who gives me strength." (Philippians 4:13)

- **You are protected.** "If the Lord delights in a man's way, he makes his steps firm; though he stumble, he will not fall, for the Lord upholds him with his hand." (Psalm 37:23–24)
- **You are God's handiwork and He is working in you.** "He who began a good work in you will carry it on to completion until the day of Christ Jesus." (Philippians 1:6)

Jesus knows you intimately. He knows exactly who you are because He lovingly created you in His image. He knows your entire story and has a plan all worked out to take your jagged and battered pieces, renew them, and reshape them. You don't have to figure it out by yourself. All that's required is that you learn to trust Jesus to "teach [you] wisdom in the inmost place," to "test [you] and know [your] anxious thoughts," to "see if there is any offensive way in [you], and lead [you] in the way everlasting" (Psalm 51:6; Psalm 139:23–24; emphasis added).

As you try to figure out who you are and sort through the jumbled notes that make up your life's song, you can be confident that Jesus already sees and intimately knows how all of the pieces fit together. He's eager to teach you how all of those black splotches on the page you're currently viewing can flow through Him and eventually reach a satisfying climax.

Right now, you might see the worst in yourself. So does Jesus. The difference is that He also sees the best in you that He has created you to be! The apostle Paul tells us this in Romans 15:4.

> For everything that was written in the past was written to teach us, so that through endurance and the encouragement of the Scriptures we might have hope.

Although Jesus waited forty years to reveal to me the wounds and mistaken beliefs surrounding my grandpa's death, He remained quite busy teaching me a multitude of other painfully important lessons.

As you learn to trust Jesus, He will continue His work of changing your heart and mind and maturing you into His own image. With Jesus at your side and His Word in your mind, who you are in Jesus *today* is always enough!

Chapter 3

What Are You Feeling?

We're continually bombarded by sights and sounds and situations that can trigger a variety of feelings. Because I'm an animal lover and once had a gentle Maltese puppy of my own, a picture or video of a cute, frolicking puppy quickly triggers a smile and a giggle as I remember the playful antics of my sweet Muffin. Sadly, one of those TV ads from the Animal Humane Society playing somber music and showing abused and abandoned animals brings a river of tears and elicits in me a deep feeling of distress and anger as I ponder the irresponsibility of some people.

It may seem that you're being controlled by your feelings. Whether or not you acknowledge them, feelings often result in some type of thoughtless response or behavior. Many people seek counseling because they're having feelings they'd rather not have, such as depression, anxiety, or uncontrolled anger, and because of the effect the expression of those feelings is having on their work and relationships.

You may not have been taught as a child how to identify or cope with your feelings. Most of us grew up feeling things we often didn't understand and, if we were bold enough to express those feelings, we could only watch the reactions of the people around us to learn what was or was not acceptable behavior. Because we didn't have the knowledge or skills to sort out the various messages we received from teachers, parents, pastors, and others in authority, we were unable to discern whether or not those messages were the truth. As a result, we grew up confused and conflicted by the wide range of "truths" that we observed and were taught about how to be.

At some point, someone has probably told you, "You shouldn't feel that way." When you do feel that way, you want to crawl in a hole because you learned at an early age that feeling what you shouldn't feel is clearly bad, or at least not normal or acceptable. Now as an adult, you spend a great deal of time and energy controlling or stuffing your emotions, defending your reactions, or trying to deny that your feelings even exist.

As a young teen, I felt lonely, unloved, and abandoned. One day I was standing in the living room of our family home and crying for no particular reason. Looking back now, I suspect that I was acting out my sense that nobody really loved me or cared about me. Mom came into the room, and the only thing I remember her saying was, "You'd better pull yourself together." Then she turned and walked away. She didn't take me in her arms and hold me; she didn't ask me what I was crying about. At least, that's the way I remembered it. I decided right then that crying was a bad thing because it caused the people I depended on to walk away from me and leave me all alone in my sadness. From that day on, I did everything I could to hide my tears, usually by escaping into a book, playing the piano, watching TV, or going off by myself, where at least I could cry without being scolded or abandoned.

For years I was hesitant to cry in front of people for fear of being shamed or scolded. I was already in my fifties when I was finally assured by a therapist that it really is okay to cry.

Do you think crying is a shameful thing? You likely learned that untruth at a time when you were in a vulnerable position. Everyone in this world has reasons to cry; life is difficult and can be extremely painful. When you break a bone in your body, you cry out in pain. When someone you dearly love dies, you weep in grief because the place in your heart that was filled with that person's love now feels empty. When a baby takes her first breath of this world's air, she immediately starts to cry—loudly! She can sense immediately that she's no longer in a safe, warm place, and she's probably experiencing her first throbbing headache. "Put me back!" she screams. There's more than enough pain to go around in this world, and pain of any kind can bring a torrent of tears.

- When you start to cry, do you look around to make sure nobody's watching? What are you afraid they'll see?
- When do you believe it's okay to show your sadness or despair? When you're grieving a loss? When you're frightened? When you're lost in a strange place? When you're not feeling well?

- Why do you think it's okay to cry at certain times but not at others?
- What do you think might happen when you cry publicly or privately?

While I was experiencing those "I'm invisible" feelings during my teenage years, the fear of rejection and abandonment incessantly haunted me. I became afraid to ask for anything from anyone—a hug, a one-on-one conversation, a shoulder to cry on—for fear I'd be turned away or rebuffed with words like "You need to pull yourself together," "I don't have time," or "You shouldn't feel that way." I was certain that asking and not receiving would hurt more than not asking and remaining in need.

Hiding Places

When you feel ashamed or unloved, you try to hide your feelings, deny them, or ignore them. Sometimes you try to shut down your emotions with mind-numbing drugs, alcohol, or food. You may engage in other distractions such as television or computer games believing that if you don't listen, don't see, don't hear, and don't think, you also won't feel. You can become frantically busy, becoming a workaholic, shopping daily, and signing up for every volunteer opportunity available just to keep yourself active but not feeling. When you're depressed, you can become almost catatonic because you're trying so hard not to feel anything.

Brené Brown, researcher, author, and TED Talk speaker, calls this numbing our feelings. She states, "We cannot selectively numb emotions; when we numb the painful emotions, we also numb the positive emotions."[10]

When you eventually discover that trying to not feel hasn't stopped the feelings, then you begin doing everything you can to protect yourself from the shaming messages that are buzzing around your head. You become a perfectionist, keeping everything around you spotless or obsessing over every mistake you make. You start building a thick wall around your feelings that you can hide behind. Each time you feel broken or betrayed and hear those shaming messages that you're useless or unloved, you set another brick in place. Those bricks can be labeled loser, complainer, despondent, guilty, obstinate, weak, or insecure. Each new brick in your wall adds another layer to your isolation and speeds up that downward spiral into depression. And there you hide, alone, sad, hopeless, and numb.

You probably have responsibilities that scream for your time and energy, so you whitewash the outside of your jagged wall and cover it with the word _Fine_. This often becomes your first line of defense: when someone asks "How are you?" you say "I'm fine." You have no intention of revealing your true feelings because of the imagined danger you might face from your well-meaning friends who try to break through your carefully built hiding place with shallow advice or shaming reprimands. Each time you answer "Fine" from behind your wall, you don't want them to know that what you really mean is that you're "**Feeling Incompetent, Needy, and Empty.**"

- You present a false picture of yourself by posting smiling selfies on Facebook right after you've had a fierce argument with your spouse, your boss, or your best friend.
- You go out to lunch with acquaintances and pretend you like who they may be pretending to be so you will feel included and wanted.
- You get hooked on texting or tweeting or internet surfing so you can pretend you don't notice the awful stuff happening around you.
- You allow individuals whom you either admire or fear to control your life so you can pretend that your bad choices are their fault, not yours.
- You pretend to have an insurmountable problem in the hope that someone will take a break from their busyness to sit with and listen to you.
- If all else fails, you escape into sleep.

I did my hiding behind the piano. Not literally; I didn't scrunch down under the Steinway grand at church and pretend I wasn't there. I did use my work at the piano as a hiding place for my tender psyche. Because that large instrument physically separated me from the choir and other orchestra members, I was easily able to isolate myself and continue my comfortable role as an introvert.

I spent a significant portion of my life hiding behind my musical wall, not allowing my unwelcome feelings or thoughts to escape or be revealed, always trying to keep people at arm's length. I was afraid to expose or confront my feelings, which were filled with contradictions.

The problem with building a wall so high that other people can't get inside is that you also can't get outside where the sunshine, laughter, and true friends are. Thus, you have to put on a mask to pretend you're socially acceptable, and you only slip out from behind that mask occasionally to have minimal, though cautious, interaction with the human race.

My Secret Room

Today, I feel strangely uncomfortable as I enter my secret room to rest and enjoy my treasures. Though none of my friends are aware of this safe place where I hide, I'm painfully aware that Jesus knows my heart and sees all. So why doesn't He force me to clean out this room and move out? He asks for nothing and offers no rebuke. Instead, He stands quietly outside the door so that each time I enter, I must first pass by Him, averting my eyes from the probing light of His holy presence.

What was it the preacher read yesterday? Something from First John: "If we claim to have fellowship with Him yet walk in the darkness, we lie and do not live by the truth."[11]

"But," I protest, "it's not that simple!" Once again, I shrug off the obvious questions and quickly close the door behind me so the light of His Truth cannot penetrate the darkness of my secret room.

Jesus will never force His way into your secret room. He'll patiently wait for you to reach for His hand through that small slit in the wall where His light and grace are peeking through.

Why Are You Hiding?

One weekend, while sitting in my comfy chair and reading a book, Jesus tapped me on the head and asked, "Why are you hiding?"

"What? It's Saturday! I'm enjoying a quiet day at home with a good book and some relaxing music. I'm not hiding—*You* found me, didn't You?"

Since being sarcastic with the Lord never got me anywhere, I closed my book and started to think about the different ways I hide.

- The first one was easy: I'm an introvert. I prefer to be alone where I can focus on my ideas, my books, my music ... oh, yes, and the Lord.
- The second was also easy: I enjoy my independence. No boss to tell me what to do; no husband for whom I must compromise my time and energies; being able to go where I want and when I want; and being able to take care of most of my daily needs without asking for help.
- The third is related to my stubbornness. I'm reluctant to accept advice from anyone. I tend to become defensive if someone tries to guide my thinking or offer a suggestion. Obviously, that made therapy a real challenge for me and for my therapist!

As I tried to understand what Jesus meant by hiding, He reminded me that I had left a number of people behind when I moved away from the large church community to which I was so closely tied. "Throughout your life, since you were a child, I've placed specific people in your path to provide the emotional and psychological support you've needed. Those are the people you were able to develop deep connection with and who stuck with you through your long years of depression as you struggled to understand life. Don't throw that away!"

I started thinking about some of those people who have been precious to me: a pastor in my hometown who was willing to sit and talk with me throughout my growing up years; a college friend who I immediately connected with and have remained in touch with for over fifty years; another pastor and his wife, who were much like a second father and mother to me; a mentor from church who came alongside me and showed me the grace and compassion of Jesus; a church organist whose company I enjoyed because we shared our love of music, and he made me laugh; and a Christian therapist who is now a dear friend and encourager.

With only a couple of exceptions, I had gradually stopped spending time with these individuals, although I still thought of them often. Why did I do that? I was trying to prove to myself and everyone else that I was now a grown-up who could manage life on her own. I was hiding behind my false pride and avoiding those people who would clearly see through my deception.

I decided to jot down the names of those people I recognized as the ones Jesus had deliberately placed in my path to hold me up, hold me accountable, and keep me safe, right up to the present time. I was able to name several people who have been and still are important to me and with whom I still have deep connection.

Instead of maintaining regular contact with those people, I'd been trying to develop all new connections in my new church home. Unfortunately, I wasn't looking for Jesus' hand in the process. I was following the suggestions of those in my new circle of acquaintances to go to this event with them and their friends, or to go out to eat after church with this or that small group—the very things that depressed introverts abhor! Each time I did one of those things, I went home feeling lonelier than ever, like a disconnected Lego or a fifth wheel. Although I was present with the group, I felt invisible. The people seated next to me were busy talking to their already established friends. I don't do well with small talk, so I had no idea what to say to get someone to notice my presence among them. The questioning of my worth started all over again.

- What's wrong with me?
- Why are relationships so hard for me?
- Why do I hold people at arm's length and not allow them to get too close to my heart?
- What am I hiding?

In my sadness and uncertainty, I quickly reverted to my ingrained habit of acting excessively needy and clingy to obtain the care and comfort I craved from those precious few people who have stuck with me.

For a significant period of time, I wouldn't allow myself to get close to Jesus because His presence always put me in touch with my fear and confusion, and He exposed deep pain I didn't want to face. Whenever I sensed discomfort and shame pressing in on me and tears threatening to give me away, I would quickly shut Him out by escaping into the world of music and books, always keeping my fingers and mind busy.

There is a better solution! You don't have to stay hidden behind your wall or go on pretending that you're someone you like. God is well aware of your need to hide from your fears, shame, and rejection. He has provided these comforting and encouraging words in the psalms of David.

> The Lord is a refuge for the oppressed, a stronghold in times of trouble. (Psalm 9:9)

> He will cover you with his feathers, and under his wings you will find refuge. (Psalm 91:4)

> You are my hiding place; you will protect me from trouble and surround me with songs of deliverance. (Psalm 32:7)

All that is required is that you seek Him out. As you seek shelter under His wings and rest from your anxiety and pain, He can teach you to acknowledge and name your feelings and then find healthier ways to respond to them instead of just reacting or hiding.

Name Your Feelings

Although there are hundreds of words that describe different nuances of feelings, we tend to use only general terms such as sad or angry to describe what we're really experiencing. In order to get in touch with our feelings and deal with them wisely, it's important to give them specific names to more clearly recognize their full impact.

For example, I could say I'm upset by what Mr. B said to me. More specifically, if I say I feel devalued by Mr. B's comments, then I suddenly touch that long-standing childhood belief that I'm not good enough.

Instead of saying you feel angry, try to identify whether the feeling relates more to annoyance, betrayal, or bitterness. Instead of saying you feel hurt, try to use a more specific word such as humiliated or offended.

Once you're able to more clearly define the feeling, it will be much easier to uncover the messages behind it and talk yourself through it.

Below is a greatly abbreviated list of feelings that can help you understand how a more specific word for what you're feeling can shed light on the true meaning of your situation. To find more words defining feelings, go to the internet and type in "Feelings Vocabulary Chart."

Feelings Chart

Afraid	Confused	Happy	Sad
Alarmed	Ambivalent	Amused	Dejected
Apprehensive	Baffled	Delighted	Disappointed
Defensive	Bewildered	Exuberant	Discouraged
Desperate	Dazed	Giddy	Forlorn
Guarded	Disorganized	Pleased	Heavy-hearted
Intimidated	Flustered	Radiant	Miserable
Panicky	Mixed-up	Rapturous	Melancholy
Shaken	Puzzled	Tickled	Weepy
Angry	**Doubtful**	**Hurt**	**Tense**
Aggravated	Distrustful	Abused	Anxious
Enraged	Dubious	Aching	Cranky
Furious	Hesitant	Crushed	Distressed
Hostile	Indecisive	Heartbroken	Distraught
Incensed	Perplexed	Insulted	Edgy
Offended	Skeptical	Mistreated	Fidgety
Spiteful	Suspicious	Put Down	Irritable
Vindictive	Uncertain	Rejected	Nervous
Annoyed	**Involved**	**Numb**	**Uneasy**
Dismayed	Absorbed	Aloof	Agitated
Disgruntled	Alert	Apathetic	Alarmed
Displeased	Curious	Bored	Disturbed
Exasperated	Enchanted	Detached	Rattled
Frustrated	Engrossed	Distant	Restless
Impatient	Fascinated	Distracted	Startled
Irritated	Intrigued	Indifferent	Troubled
Irked	Stimulated	Withdrawn	Unnerved

Ashamed	Fatigued	Peaceful	Insecure
Apologetic	Burned out	Calm	Fragile
Awkward	Depleted	Confident	Guarded
Defective	Exhausted	Content	Helpless
Embarrassed	Lethargic	Mellow	Leery
Guilty	Listless	Relaxed	Reserved
Humiliated	Tired	Serene	Sensitive
Incompetent	Weary	Tranquil	Shaky

Control Your Feelings

There is no right or wrong way to feel. Your feelings are what they are, and you can't control their existence any more than you can control your physical reflexes.

Do you remember that time when you were driving down the highway, and suddenly a bird swooped at your windshield? What did you do? You ducked! Did you think about ducking? Of course not; that was your body's involuntary response to an unexpected threat. You only thought about it seconds later, and then you wondered why in the world you ducked because you were protected by a thick windshield. You ducked because you couldn't stop that automatic, physical reflex to being suddenly startled. Fortunately, that bird couldn't stop its automatic reflex to veer off, thereby saving both himself and your windshield!

To a certain degree, the same is true of feelings. You can't avoid feeling any more than you can avoid ducking when something flies at your face. Your feelings are a basic, spontaneous reaction to what's happening around you and within you.

Whether you're aware of it or not, your feelings generate a physical reflex in your body. When you feel afraid, angry, frustrated, or stubborn, your body stiffens and feels uptight. When you feel cheerful, relieved, or confident, your body feels more relaxed.

- Have you ever felt your muscles tense up, your face heat up, and your heart rate increase? Your body could be reacting to your anger.
- Do you shuffle slowly along with your head and shoulders slumped forward? Your body may be reacting to your sadness or discomfort.

- Are your hands or legs trembling? Are your eyes dilated? Are you suddenly feeling a headache? Your body could be reacting to fear or extreme stress.

(Note: These are common examples that aren't limited to these specific emotions.)

Lesson #1 in Brain Chemistry

There's a radical difference between your physical reflexes and your emotional reactions.

- A physical reflex is involuntary, like the sudden blinking of your eyelids when a piece of dirt or sudden blast of air hits them.
- An emotional reaction is voluntary. It can be controlled.

But wait! If your feelings are spontaneously generated, how can they also be voluntary and controllable?

A physical reflex like ducking actually bypasses the brain and doesn't involve any conscious reasoning. Instead, the sensory nerves send a message directly to the central nervous system and then quickly back to the motor nerves. You don't have to think about snatching your hand away when it touches a hot stove. Your sensory and motor nerves do it for you.

On the other hand, an emotional reaction causes your sensory nerves to carry the information directly to the brain, not to the central nervous system. The brain then sends a message telling the motor nerves to respond to the stimulus. An emotional reaction isn't just an unthinking reflex to a stimulus, like a knee jerking when the doctor hits it with a rubber mallet. An emotional reaction directly involves your brain.

In my research on feelings and brain activity, I was fascinated to discover that feelings are actually like a two-sided coin. On one side of the coin is your initial feeling and reaction to a comment or situation. On the flip side of the coin is your response to that feeling! Because your brain is quickly working to engage additional nerves besides your sensory nerves, there's usually a split second of time available between your initial reaction and your response.

That's good news! While your brain is involved in reacting to feelings, a thought is triggered that you aren't immediately aware of, and you have a split-second chance to flip the coin, stop your reaction, and think about what you're feeling.

I love to watch tennis even though I don't play the game myself. I'm always amazed to see how quickly a player reacts to a little yellow ball that's coming at him at over a hundred miles per hour. How is that even possible? Well, as soon as he hears the ball hit the opponent's racquet, his sensory nerves immediately engage his central nervous system, causing his arm, shoulder, and leg muscles to tense up. Then, in that split second when his eyes see the ball flying toward him, his sensory nerves directly engage his brain, which instantaneously processes his options: (1) Should I hit a lob into the air to allow more time to reposition myself for the next volley? (2) Should I try a drop shot to surprise my opponent? (3) Should I hit a hard backhand shot to the right to throw off my opponent's choice of direction? A well-trained player who's paying attention won't react with a wild swing. Instead, he will consciously control his muscles, take a purposeful swing, and hopefully hit the ball into the corner!

God has designed our intricate brains so that we only need a split-second flip of the coin to scroll through all of the ideas, memories, and beliefs we've stored away and to choose the appropriate response, thus changing the outcome, whether we're interacting with another person or with a fast-moving tennis ball.

When I was in college, I experienced this flip-of-the-coin process in a unique way. The college choir was presenting its annual fall concert, with hundreds of family members, friends, and college faculty in attendance. I was at the piano as the only instrumentalist. As we performed a particular piece, we were all alert and watching the director carefully so we wouldn't miss a single cue. The song was building, building, building ... then just as we belted out a strong, climactic chord, all the lights in the auditorium went out! But the song wasn't finished yet! There was still one final phrase to perform.

I didn't know what was happening with the choir on stage at that moment, but I had abruptly shifted into "fight or flight" mode. My heart skipped a beat, and my eyes opened wide because I suddenly couldn't see the music in front of me or the director on the stage. My automatic sensory reflex lifted my hands off the keyboard as if it were a hot stove. Fortunately, the whole choir stopped singing at exactly the same moment. Their sensory reflexes apparently shut their mouths!

In that split second, my immediate thought and instant response was to move my fingers into position for the next chord and turn my head in the direction where I had last seen the director before the room went dark. Surprisingly, the lights came back on just six or seven seconds later. At the hasty downbeat of our director's baton, we all started in unison and flawlessly finished the piece. The transition was so smooth that the audience could easily have believed the startling darkness was cunningly planned for dramatic effect. I'm sure the look of shock on all of our faces gave it away: there was no plan—just plenty of drama! That had to be a one-of-a-kind miracle from the Lord, and He nailed it! He had blessed each of us with the same thought in that unexpected moment of darkness: stop and think. And the reason it worked? We were all paying attention.

> Between stimulus and response, there is a space.
> In that space is our power to choose our response.
> In our response lies our growth and our freedom.
> —Viktor E. Frankl[12]

These words explain quite well the incredible, God-created process that allows you to think about what you're feeling and then to respond appropriately and courageously.

Too often you don't take advantage of that split second to let your brain process what you're reacting to. The result is an impulsive knee-jerk or loose-tongue reaction. Those are the times when you fly off the handle and blurt out whatever comes immediately to your untamed tongue, oblivious to and unconcerned about the consequences. An impulsive emotional reaction isn't usually appropriate because it can turn an already tense situation into a confrontation where serious harm or uncontrollable chaos can result. In the case of the college choir, we could have ended up with a horrible cacophony of clashing notes and no rational rhythm!

A Shameful Moment in Time

When your reaction is impulsive, you usually end up saying something that you later deeply regret. I learned that painful lesson as a young and quite immature adult in a particularly icy confrontation with my dad.

In those difficult days when I was still trying to protect myself from the awful feelings of being unloved and useless, I didn't want anyone, especially my dad, telling me what to do. As a result, I allowed my still adolescent feelings to rule my behavior. Whenever Dad tried to help me, I unknowingly translated his gestures or words to mean that I was inept, or stupid, or not good enough—and I defended myself with anger or defiance.

One weekend I had driven home to Iowa for a short visit. It was winter in the Midwest, and a nasty storm had blown through Iowa and deposited a thick coating of ice on my car, which was parked in the backyard of my parents' home. This Sunday afternoon, I needed to drive back to Minneapolis so I could make it to my job on Monday morning.

Like all hardy Midwesterners, I bundled up against the frigid north wind and went out the back door to begin the work of chopping and scraping the stubborn ice off my car windows. While I was totally absorbed in this task, I didn't notice that Dad had come outside and gone to the garage for something. Suddenly there he was beside me, holding a propane torch, like the ones people use to light the charcoal in a grill. Much to my chagrin, he lit the thing and pointed it at my car!

Clearly this college graduate thought she was smarter than her dad, and I immediately shouted at him. "What are you doing? You're going to burn the paint!" I was dumbfounded that he thought a torch was a good solution. Of course, his only intention was to melt the ice on the windshield, not torch my car. But my frozen brain could only think, *He doesn't believe I can do this by myself,* and I behaved accordingly.

The damage had been done—not to my car, but to Dad's heart. He quickly turned off the torch, stored it away in the garage, and silently walked back into the house, leaving me to my feeble efforts to chop the ice off my car and bring my outrage under control. I finished the scraping job in a short time, but thawing out my hardened ego took many years.

Although I'm not eager to tell you the rest of the story, that wouldn't be honest or helpful. The truth is that Jesus recently resurrected this long-lost memory and encouraged me to relive the fullness of that devastating moment in time.

When I went back in the house that cold afternoon, Mom was waiting for me in the kitchen. Dad had already removed his coat and hat and was sitting quietly in the living room. Mom softly said to me, "Your dad was just trying to help." I was in such a sullen mood that I didn't hear her words as a plea for understanding or gratitude. Instead, I heard a reprimand that caused my anger to flare once again. I spit out some ugly words and fled upstairs to my bedroom. I finished packing up my things, flounced down the steps, and announced, "I'm heading home now. Bye." When my rattled emotions finally settled down several miles later, I stuffed that incident into my "never mind" basket of memories and refused to think of it again. That ugly moment was eventually buried and lost.

As Jesus walked me back through that awful scene, I felt ashamed and disgusted by my appalling attitude and behavior toward Dad. I began scolding myself for being such a stupid girl back then. When I looked into Jesus' eyes, I immediately began to weep. I felt deeply remorseful as I realized when that horrible exchange took place between me and Dad, something in our relationship broke, and neither of us seemed to know how to fix it. We didn't know how to say, "I'm sorry."

Thankfully, at some point during Dad's final days with us, he and I were both able to speak the most important words: "I love you." Unfortunately, those belated words didn't resolve the years of anger and stubborn pride that had resulted in that high wall of nervous tension that grew between us. I deeply regret not being able to chop away enough of my icy pride to speak and act out those healing words much earlier in life. Things could have been quite different between us because I really did love Dad. He was a solid Christian man, a good father, and a wonderful provider for his family. My heart aches at the knowledge that I was too obstinate to ever tell him that. As I stood at the foot of his hospital bed after he had taken his final breath, I could only think *You should have said something.* But it was too late. He was gone, and I couldn't take back those angry words and stubborn attitudes I had displayed so frequently while he was alive.

It doesn't take any effort at all to react to every emotion that comes your way. When you're simply reacting, you always seem to be on the defensive or on the edge of aggression. When you're uncomfortable with something that's being said or done, and you react out of anger, frustration, shame, or foolishness, your brain is disengaged and your ability to reason is aborted. This can cause a precious relationship to be irreparably damaged or completely destroyed.

However, it is possible to stop an impulsive emotional reaction, make a wise choice, and quietly respond. The key is to take advantage of that split second to engage your brain and make a different choice in how you will respond to what you're feeling. I wonder now what would have happened if I had stopped my tongue for a couple seconds and simply asked Dad if he was sure the torch wouldn't burn anything. I could have kept quiet and trusted him to know what he was doing. Perhaps we could have joked about it later, turning it into a funny, endearing memory. Sadly, those options are no longer mine to choose. I can only remember and weep now—and ask the Lord to forgive me.

Once you understand that feelings contribute to who you are and learn how to engage and manage those feelings, then brick by brick you can finally begin dismantling your wall and open your heart to the healing power of Jesus and the joy of healthier relationships with others.

On Feelings

Part 1
To feel only joy is unrealistic.
To feel only pain is inhuman.
To feel only anger is pathetic.
To feel only forgiveness is pretense.
To feel only need is selfish.
To feel needed is an uncertainty.
To feel only love is idealistic.
To feel only hate is unchristian.
To feel only lust is immoral.
To feel only pride is sinful.
To feel nothing is unbearable.
But to feel each of these at some time
during the human experience is *life*.

Learning to Lament

What can you do with your nameless anger, your physical suffering, your emotional agony, and your frustrated questioning? Where can you go when your heart is breaking and all you can ask is "Why Lord?"

Our world tells us to "just deal with it" when life hurls us into a dark pit and holds us down. Even our churches counsel us that we must meet life's unexplained pain and difficulties with joy. We go to our "happy place" or hide behind our "Fine" wall in efforts to stuff and ignore the deep sorrow, or the burning anger, or the agonizing despair of life in this broken world. Unfortunately, all of our pretending disengages us not only from people but also from God.

God wants to show you a better way. Scripture is filled with lament. Dictionaries define lament as "feeling or expressing sorrow or grief." Although this isn't a word that's used much these days, it's important in the process of healing wounds of the heart inflicted on you by this world and by your own faulty thinking.

Over one-third of the psalms are laments. One of those psalms was used by Jesus as He agonized on the cross: "My God, my God, why have you forsaken me ...?" (Psalm 22:1). The laments sprinkled throughout scripture are addressed directly to God. Job complained, "Why did I not perish at birth ...?" (Job 3:11). The prophet Jeremiah cried out to God: "Why is my pain unending and my wound grievous and incurable ...?" (Jeremiah 15:18). The psalmist pleaded: "Why, Lord, do you stand far off? Why do you hide yourself in times of trouble?" (Psalm 10:1).

Your suffering is often so deep that it doesn't make any sense, and you're afraid to expose it to the light of honesty. As a Christian, you may be uncomfortable expressing your pain, your anger, or your doubts to God. You're afraid of lament, believing you "shouldn't feel this way." You think that to complain to God is to show no trust in Him—but that's not biblical.

In her book *No More Faking Fine,*[13] Esther Fleece provides this explanation.

Lament is the constructive way to deal with our seemingly uncontrollable feelings. When we lament, we come face to face with God as we try to understand what is happening in our hearts. Lament isn't the same as despair. To despair is to lose all hope. In despair we give up on our relationship with God. Lamenting over our doubts and struggles is a sign that our faith in God's presence and power is still alive. In lamenting, we are wrestling with Him, trusting our entire being to Him as we seek meaningful answers to our bottomless sorrow.

Chris Tiegreen wrote these comforting words in his book *Why a Suffering World Makes Sense.*

God may seem silent in our suffering, but He longs for us to reach out to Him in our need, throw our anger and bitterness in His lap, scream to Him about our agony and grief, beg Him for help and mercy, lie weak and helpless in His arms, and let Him weep for us. It's in those moments of your naked laments and helpless trust that He is eager and able to wrap you in His strong arms of Love and begin showing you the reality of His nearness.[14]

When you invite God into your suffering, He doesn't necessarily change your situation or relieve your agony. He does change you from the inside as He displays His presence and fills you with His peace. He assures you that He is always with you regardless of the circumstances. When you run to God with your sorrow and skepticism, He weeps with you and changes your perspective—about Himself and about the eternal hope He provides.

Silent God

You say I'm a silent God,
yet you haven't asked Me to speak.
I've been here all along, watching you, loving you,
waiting patiently for the moment
when you would be ready
to cry out to Me and listen to My voice.
I've longed for you to share with Me your tears,
allowing Me the privilege of weeping with you.

You've struggled alone for so long, My child,
fearing that I would not accept your bitter shouts of anger
or hear your pleading cries for comfort.
I feel the anguish of your downcast thoughts.
I moan over the desolation of your spirit.
I long for you to hand Me the pieces of your broken heart
and allow Me to heal them and seal them together
with the sweet balm of My everlasting love.

I will always be here for you, precious one.
Be not afraid ... and be no longer silent.

There is much to gain by learning from the psalmists how to lament.

How long, Lord? Will you forget me forever? How long
will you hide your face from me? How long must I
wrestle with my thoughts and day after day have sorrow
in my heart? How long will my enemy triumph over me?
(Psalm 13:1–2)

Turn to me and be gracious to me, for I am lonely and
afflicted. Relieve the troubles of my heart and free me
from my anguish. Look on my affliction and my distress

and take away all my sins. See how numerous are my enemies and how fiercely they hate me! Guard my life and rescue me; do not let me be put to shame, for I take refuge in you. (Psalm 25:16–20)

Write down some of your complaints and "why" questions.

- What difficulties and challenges are you facing right now?
- What pain or remorse do you feel?
- What anger or confusion is blocking your relationship with the Lord?

Bring those things directly to Him and allow Him to talk you through them. He will stand with you in your moments of lament and reveal to you a deeper understanding of His presence.

What Does God Think about Feelings?

God made you in His own image, and that includes the whole range of emotions that are a vital part of who He is. God is a feeling God. He feels sadness, He exhibits anger, He enjoys laughter, and He offers compassion and delight. God is love! When God created this amazing world, including humans, the angels shouted for joy (Job 38:7). He wants you to experience the joy of His salvation (Psalm 51:12) and the peace of His Spirit, which you can only begin to comprehend in this life (Philippians 4:7).

If you were to do a study of emotions in the Bible, you would discover that feelings are rampant in God's Word! The following paraphrased verses provide a few examples of what God says about feelings.

- **Delight.** "Delight yourself in the Lord and he will give you the desires of your heart." (Psalm 37:4)
- **Affection.** "Be devoted to one another in brotherly love." (Romans 12:10)
- **Joy.** "You have pain now; but I will see you again and your hearts will rejoice, and no one will take your joy from you." (John 16:22)
- **Fear.** "Do not be terrified; do not be discouraged, for the Lord your God will be with you wherever you go." (Joshua 1:9)

- **Self-control.** "Like a city whose walls are broken down is a man who lacks self-control." (Proverbs 25:28)
- **Confusion.** "God is not a God of disorder but of peace." (1 Corinthians 14:33)
- **Mixed Feelings.** "There is a time for everything ... a time to weep and a time to laugh." (Ecclesiastes 3:1–8)

How are you feeling now? Encouraged, I hope! There are emotions that make you uneasy. You might feel bored, impatient, distressed, embarrassed, apprehensive, or anxious. There are emotions that bring color and dimension to your existence. You could feel excited, determined, confident, and cheerful. Without emotions, life would be rather blah. You would be like a living, breathing robot! Naturally, you would rather do without the painful emotions like anger, shame, bitterness, or insecurity. Yet those are the very emotions that can urge you to make key changes in your behavior and attitudes and draw you closer to God.

Whenever I become weary of the struggle with my feelings, I remind myself that Jesus has experienced every one of these emotions, and I was made in His image. He created me to be like Himself: full of feeling. As I listen to my favorite Christian artist, Kathy Troccoli, singing about His "Stubborn Love," I am brought to tears when I hear the truth of one eloquently poignant line: "You stay and say You love me still, knowing someday I'll be like You."[15] That's amazing grace!

There's nowhere else I'd rather be than standing in the circle of His strong arms, sensing that deep, pulsing love that burns in His heart for me, His child.

On Feelings

Part 2

To accept my feelings as being me,
to judge them neither good nor bad
but as being uniquely mine
and valuable for my here and now,
to allow them to sweep over me and through me,
and to be in touch with them
is to listen to myself
and thus become closer and freer
to being who I am.

To feel is to live.
I will learn to live with my feelings,
for to deny them is to deny myself and my God.

Chapter 4
What's on Your Mind?

Which came first: the depression or the destructive thoughts? When you focus on your pain—your unresolved difficulties, your unmet needs, your damaged relationships—it's easy to convince yourself that you've already tried everything and failed.

Depression is the body's way of defending us against the ill effects of chronic, pessimistic thinking. Without the numbing effect of depression, our bodies must deal with the constant stress response that results from our persistent and unchecked, defeatist thinking.[16] The numbing effect of depression on our emotions calms the body's chemistry. However, as previously noted, depression isn't selective in which emotions it affects; it numbs all of them, including joy and contentment.

When we're depressed we see the world through dark glasses and our thoughts become discouraging: "I'll never be worth anything." "No one could possibly love me." "I wish I'd never been born."

Think You Can or Think You Can't

On one occasion, I was whining to my therapist about a particular situation in which another person had said something that angered me. She responded by asking, "What were you thinking at the time?"

Somewhat aggravated by the question, I quickly retorted, "What's that got to do with anything?"

I've since learned that what you're thinking has everything to do with everything! Depressed or not, you may not notice your actual thoughts because you're so busy reacting to the events of your life. You carry on

55

silent conversations with yourself all day long, but your thoughts are so automatic that you don't really think about what you're thinking about.

Because you're not aware of those thoughts that whiz through your brain at the speed of light, or at the flip of a coin, you tend to expect the worst and often blame yourself with thoughts like this:

- I can't do this.
- I'm not good enough.
- My life is a mess.
- It's always my fault.
- Nothing ever changes.

There are numerous ways to consistently make errors in logic and judgment which then affect your mood. Below is an example with four possible scenarios.

Your friend has agreed to go to a movie with you but is now late. Your automatic thought and interpretation of this situation will determine how you feel and think about either your friend or yourself.

My friend is late.
    Automatic thought: I probably told her the wrong time.
    Reactive feeling: self-blame, "I'm so stupid."
My friend is late.
    Automatic thought: She's always late! Why do I put up with this?
    Reactive feeling: angry at my friend, frustrated with myself.
My friend is late.
    Automatic thought: If she valued our friendship, she'd be on time.
    Reactive feeling: ignored, insignificant, unneeded.
My friend is late.
    Automatic thought: I hope nothing has happened and she's all right.
    Reactive feeling: anxious, concerned about your friend.

When your response to a situation is focused on blaming or shaming, you eventually reach a point where it's easier to say, "I don't like how I'm feeling, but that's just the way it is; I can't do anything about it." You see no reason for hope that things will get better. You're not consciously aware that the despair and hopelessness you feel is the result of a harmful way of interpreting and responding to life experiences.

Whether you think you can or you think you can't, you're absolutely right.

—Henry Ford[17]

Often you would rather escape a situation than change your thinking (e.g., get a divorce rather than seek counseling, quit a job rather than resolve a stressful issue). Irrational thinking becomes the easy way out, and those radical decisions can severely disrupt your life, creating even more damage, mistrust, and defeat.

The key is to change the nature of your thoughts from hopeless and destructive to expectant and nurturing. Using the example just cited about waiting for your friend at the movie theater, let's say your automatic thoughts followed this track.

> Why didn't she call and tell me she would be late? I wanted to meet several minutes before the show starts so we could have some time to visit. How could she do this to me? Why doesn't she learn how to be on time?

Obviously, allowing those thoughts to fester stirs up your anger, frustration, and resentment. What can you do about it? Try applying these five questions.

Are those thoughts really true? Does your friend always arrive late to every event? Did you actually tell her you wanted some chat time before the movie?

Could you have misunderstood or misread things? Why would your friend deliberately ignore your wish to visit for a bit?

Is there another way to explain this disappointment? Find as many possible explanations as you can. Maybe she planned to be on time but received a call from her husband that she couldn't ignore. Maybe she thought the show started later and believed there would be plenty of time for visiting.

Even if your assumptions are partly true, so what? What's the worst possible outcome? You could miss out on what you believed was a perfect time for talking with your friend; or you might not be able to watch all of the previews of coming shows.

What can you do to turn this uncomfortable situation into a favorable opportunity?

- When your friend arrives, you can greet her warmly and ask respectfully if something happened to delay her arrival.
- You can suggest to your friend that you meet her for lunch one day soon to have some quality time to talk.
- The next time you schedule a movie date, you can remind your friend what time the movie starts and what time to meet there.

Thoughts Are Mental Events

When you become mindful of your thoughts, you will realize that both your circumstances and your thoughts are constantly changing. Your thoughts can be influenced by stress, the weather, the kind of prescription drugs you're taking, how much coffee you've had, or the aftermath of that morning argument you had with your spouse. If you begin to view your thoughts as fluid events that are happening in your brain rather than as absolute truths requiring immediate action, then you can begin to evaluate your feelings and thoughts together to help you make different decisions.

Lesson #2 in Brain Chemistry

When you're thinking, electrical impulses in your brain enable neurons to connect. These form what looks like a tree in your brain. The more you repeat the same kind of thinking, such as angry thoughts, the tree grows larger with more neurons connected to one another, and those connections grow thicker and stronger. Scientists have been able to observe this process through an electron microscope. These connections create paths that allow those repetitive messages to get through faster. God designed your brain to do that!

When you start replacing your dark thoughts with more pleasant thoughts on a consistent basis, new neurons and pathways are formed. The old connections will continually grow weaker, and that old tree will gradually disappear.[18]

Scientists have observed that dark, destructive thoughts have a damaging effect on your physical health by releasing bad chemicals into your body. Your internal system is not wired to cope with thoughts such as bitterness, judgment, resentment, self-pity, or unforgiveness. When this type of thinking persists, those neuron trees release a stream of damaging chemicals into your system that continues to grow more potent, thus overloading your immune system. Your self-destructive thinking can literally make you sick!

Capture Your Thoughts

Do you remember those warm summer nights when the sun had gone down and twilight brought out a swarm of fireflies? (In Iowa, we call them lightning bugs.) It was fun to watch them and marvel at their ability to light up their own path and communicate with each other.

Your thoughts can be as elusive as a firefly on a dark night because those moments when you can catch them are fleeting. Yet God instructs us to capture our thoughts and bring them into line with His Truth.

> We demolish arguments and every pretension that sets itself up against the knowledge of God, and we take captive every thought to make it obedient to Christ. (2 Corinthians 10:5)

What does that mean? We must stop, examine our thoughts one by one, and take active control of them. We must think about what we think about. That seems like an impossible task. It has been estimated that the average person has anywhere from twenty-five thousand to fifty thousand thoughts a day, up to five thousand thoughts an hour—and thousands of those thoughts totally escape our awareness!

However, with some vigilance we can learn to catch and identify our thoughts and either accept or refute them. When we repeatedly disprove the validity of certain thoughts, they will slowly diminish and be replaced by more rational thinking and beliefs.

> A thought is harmless unless we believe it.
> —Byron Katie[19]

Are Those Thoughts Really True?

Some of those speculations and lofty things that inhabit our thinking patterns are what psychologists call cognitive distortions. Our minds are able to convince us of something that isn't really true, even when these distorted thoughts appear rational.

American psychiatrist Aaron Beck[20] was the first to propose the theory behind cognitive distortions in 1976. Then in the 1980s, Dr. David Burns, the author of *Feeling Good: The New Mood Therapy*,[21] popularized the theory with common names and examples. Other resources are available online under "cognitive distortions" or "distorted thinking." One resource recommended to parents for teaching their children about irrational thinking is *Captain Snout and the Powerful Questions* by Dr. Daniel Amen.[22]

Below is a compilation of many of the common styles of distorted thinking, which I've gleaned from various sources.

All-or-nothing thinking. You look at things in absolute black-or-white, good-or-bad categories, with very little room for a middle ground.
Example: If your performance falls short of perfect, you see yourself as a total failure. I'm a piano player who used to think that if I didn't play a piece perfectly, I was a failure, and I'd tell myself, *You'll never be good enough.*
"Should" statements. You believe you and others should act according to certain rules. When you tell yourself you should or shouldn't have said or done something, the result is a feeling of guilt. When you find fault with what someone else said or did, the result is anger or frustration. Cue phrases are *should, ought, must,* and *have to.*
Example: I should have gone to the movie with her. I'm just selfish.
Example: The doctor is running late. I think, *As much as I'm paying him, he should be prompt and have more respect for my time.*
Filtered thinking. You tend to magnify the hostile or judgmental comments, but you reject the encouraging, honest affirmations, insisting they somehow don't count.
Example: At the end of a church service, someone complimented me on the great job I'd done at the piano. It was hard for me to accept the compliment because all I could think about was my one

conspicuously loud and glaring mistake, which caught the attention of the pastor.

Overgeneralizing. You assume that if it was true once, it's likely to be true all the time. *Always* and *never* are common cues to this kind of thinking.

Example: Linda claims she will never shop at that store again because they never have the items she needs.

Catastrophizing. You arbitrarily predict things will turn out badly. You start worrying about the what-ifs.

Example: "I've already made a mistake on this report, and I'm almost out of time. Even if I finish it, it'll be so full of mistakes it won't matter. I'll be fired no matter what."

Jumping to conclusions. You reach a judgmental conclusion even though there are no definite facts supporting your interpretation of events.

Example: You're waiting for your date who is twenty minutes late. You tell yourself you must have done something wrong, and now he has stood you up. The reality is he's stuck in traffic across town.

Emotional labeling. You mistake feelings for facts and then label yourself accordingly. Instead of describing your error, you attach a judgmental label to yourself.

Example: Instead of saying, *I made a mistake,* you label yourself a failure or an idiot. You believe that if you feel stupid or boring, then you must be stupid or boring.

Personalizing. You tend to relate everything around you to yourself. You believe what others say or do is a direct reaction to you.

Example: You see some friends talking together in a huddle. When one of them glances your way, you conclude they're talking about you.

Blaming. Blaming is the opposite of shaming. You often hold other people responsible for choices and decisions that are actually your responsibility.

Example: You're sitting in traffic when the "low fuel" light comes on. Your first angry thought is, *Why didn't my husband fill up the gas tank last night? He should have noticed it was almost empty.* When you started the car, why didn't you notice and take care of the problem yourself, without blaming your husband?

Dispute Your Thoughts

Whenever you catch yourself in a blaming or shaming thought, don't start looking for the external cause of your problems. Instead of asking who is to blame, ask, *What have I been telling myself?* Learn to engage with every single thought you have and analyze it before you decide to either accept or reject it.

Consider the following:

- How many "if only" statements were part of your inner voice today?
  If only I had kept my mouth shut.
  If only I hadn't agreed to take on that responsibility.
- How many times have you replayed in your mind a conversation or situation that caused you distress? Although you can't go back and change it, you can consider what you might say differently next time.
- How many "what if" scenarios have you created about the unpredictable future? Do they help you feel more secure, or do you worry more?
- How often do you make irrational declarations?
  This always happens to me, or, *I'll never find a job.*
  Always or *never* is a long, long time with little opportunity for change or hope!

If you hear yourself saying, "*I should ...*" try adding the word *because* in explanation.

I should clean my house once a week because people will think badly of me if they stop by and see dust and cobwebs.

Then revise your should statement by creating a more balanced and constructive statement.

I would like to clean my house once a week, but it isn't always possible.

Replace Your Thoughts

Once you get into the habit of screening and testing your thoughts, there are still going to be those moments when a self-defeating thought will creep into your mind and sit there, intruding on your mood. When that happens and you can't seem to let go of that thought, what can you do? Replace it with a different thought!

This is an old trick that usually works. Close your eyes and think about the number 23. Don't think of anything else except 23. Can you see it in big red letters in your mind? 23! Now, *stop* thinking about 23. Put 23 totally out of your mind.

Were you able to stop thinking about 23 just because I told you to? Probably not. Now, instead of thinking about 23, think of the number 78. Keep thinking about 78. Guess what? You're no longer thinking about 23 because 78 has now replaced it in your thinking.

You can use this same replacement technique with your self-defeating thoughts. If you're a follower of Christ, you have a comforting replacement thought that is guaranteed to work every time. Colossians 3:2 instructs you to "set your mind on things above." Focusing your mind on God's Word is a proven way to change your thoughts and beliefs about who you are.

How does this work? The apostle Paul provides more detailed instructions in Philippians 4:8–9.

> Finally, brothers, whatever is true, whatever is noble, whatever is right, whatever is pure, whatever is lovely, whatever is admirable—if anything is excellent or praiseworthy—think about such things.

Whatever is true—We live in a society where truth is relative. There are no absolutes. People are more concerned with feeling good than honoring what is true. Make sure you're dealing with the truth.

Whatever is noble—Noble thoughts rise above your self-interest. Once you start to think dignified and wholesome thoughts, you will stop focusing on your own circumstances and agendas.

Whatever is right—Are your thoughts fair and just? Do you tend to mentally accuse others and yourself unfairly or unjustly before verifying the facts? Practice replacing thoughts that focus on weaknesses or faults with thoughts that are complementary and right.

Whatever is pure—Do you spend a lot of time focusing on thoughts or images that stir your heart to greed or anger? You can be deeply affected by your TV viewing and internet surfing.

Whatever is lovely—Lovely thinking is caring, compassionate, and gentle. It promotes peace, not conflict. Are you protecting your mind from influences that would cause you to become controlling or critical or cause unnecessary conflict?

Whatever is admirable—Your thoughts must be in good taste and respectful. If other people could read your mind, would they admire your thoughts?[23]

What kind of nourishment are you giving your mind? What people or gadgets are you allowing to control your thinking? What kind of music do you regularly listen to? What are your TV and movie viewing habits? What kinds of books and magazines do you read? What kinds of content do you regularly view on the internet? Are you filling your mind with untrue, unholy, shameful, corrupt, and ugly thoughts?

Paul goes on to say that not only are you supposed to think about the excellent and praiseworthy things, but you are also supposed to "put it into practice." He then promises that "the God of peace will be with you." Isaiah 26:3 reminds us that God will keep in perfect peace all who trust in Him and whose thoughts are fixed on Him (paraphrase).

Take Responsibility for Your Thoughts

Simply beginning to pay attention to your thoughts doesn't mean you're immediately able to change them. Thought patterns run deep, and you often feel helpless to change them. As soon as you stop one thought, your mind generates another. Given the power of your thoughts, it becomes vitally important that you pay attention to that running inner dialogue you have with yourself; take responsibility for checking the facts and replacing the destructive thoughts with constructive thoughts.

> Be careful what you think, because your thoughts run
> your life. (Proverbs 4:23 NCV)

Changing your thinking habits can be similar to learning to play the piano: it requires practice and hard work. When I discover that I've been playing a chord or phrase of music incorrectly, I must fix the error by playing it correctly over and over until my fingers have been trained to instantly move to the correct keys. Once the chord or phrase has been ingrained in my thinking and in the response of my fingers, it then becomes difficult to play it any other way. It's a bit like riding a bicycle: once you've learned how to do it, you won't likely forget. The new skill is etched in those new pathways in your brain.

When you're trying to learn new ways of thinking and behaving, you can spend weeks and months training your brain to think a new way. Don't despair! With practice, persistence, and prayer, the new way of thinking will create new pathways in your brain and become so natural that you won't want to think any other way.

Be Creatively Content

Being content refers mostly to who you are, what you have, where you live, and how you think about life in general. Unfortunately, when you're depressed, you view yourself as a victim of the unfairness and ugliness of the world and its people, and you feel anything but content.

Following a particular church service that included a sermon on contentment, I was a bit puzzled by a friend's response to my question, *Are you content?* I thought it was odd that she would answer that question with a no, yet I, who was chronically depressed, would answer it with a yes. I looked up a few articles about contentment and Christians and found an interesting concept.

We can actually experience contentment in situations that annoy and frustrate us because our contentment as Christians is a direct result of knowing that we are each a product of God's grace in action.

We read these words in Ephesians 4:22–24.

> You were taught, with regard to your former way of life,
> to put off your old self, which is being corrupted by its
> deceitful desires; to be made new in the attitude of your
> minds; and to put on the new self, created to be like God
> in true righteousness and holiness.

After agonizing over certain life situations that continued to annoy me, I made up a new word: *GrinAct.* In my vocabulary, this stands for

"Grace in Action." When I encounter a situation that is quickly moving from annoyance to anger, I remind myself of God's grace for people like that grumpy sales clerk or the pushy, honking driver riding my bumper. In my flip-of-the-coin moment, I deliberately think differently and take an action that both calms me and surprises the offender.

- I speak a kind word to the harassed sales clerk who's clearly having a bad day.
- I refuse to honk or glare at the impatient, obnoxious driver who whips around my car and dangerously cuts in front of me.

People who act nasty are probably expecting a nasty reaction, so the look of surprise or puzzlement on their faces when I refuse to react that way puts a silly grin on my face. It gives me something fun to think about, and I can pray that the angry or frustrated individual has received a gentle lesson in patience and attitude adjustment.

Contrary to popular opinion, contentment does not mean being satisfied where you are. Rather, it is knowing that God has a plan for your life and believing that His peace is greater than the world's petty problems.

The contentment you're looking for is not impossible. The key is how you manage your thoughts. The apostle Paul wrote these brave words.

> I am not saying this because I am in need, for I have learned to be content whatever the circumstances. I know what it is to be in need, and I know what it is to have plenty. I have learned the secret of being content in any and every situation, whether well fed or hungry, whether living in plenty or in want. I can do all this through him who gives me strength. (Philippians 4:11–13)

Sincerely Repent

Have you ever done a study of the biblical word *repent*? That one word is used multiple times in the Bible, both in the Old and New Testaments. People usually think of the following when they hear the word repent.

- Feeling sorry for something they've said or done.
- Confessing wrongdoing to someone.
- Asking for forgiveness.

These are all good things to do, but none of them is about true repentance. According to scripture, "feeling sorry," "confessing," and "asking for forgiveness" are all about remorse, which is knowing you have done something wrong but having no plan or intention of making things right or changing your behavior.

- Feeling sorry distresses and isolates you, but no changes are made.
- Admitting guilt produces shame and keeps you imprisoned, but no changes are made.
- Feeling regret produces self-pity that focuses on your own pain, but no changes are made.

In Volume II of his *Sparkling Gems*[24] devotional book, Pastor Rick Renner reminds us that the Greek word for *remorse, metamelomai,* is much different than the Greek word for *repent,* which is *metanoia.* In both cases, *meta* means "turn." However:

- *lomai* refers to the emotions a person feels for doing wrong yet knowing he would continue the same behavior if he hadn't been caught.
- *noia* refers to the mind, intellect, or frame of thinking about life. When you truly repent, you're engaging your mind and will in making a deliberate change, and you're making a commitment to God to turn completely around and change the way you think and behave.

Transformed thinking results in transformed living. In Christ, you are a new person! You think differently. You act differently. You view life and the people around you differently.

As instructed in Romans 12:2, you are "to be transformed by the renewing of your mind." Guess who does the work of transforming and renewing? Jesus Christ, through the work of His Holy Spirit, who dwells in you. He's in the business of change and restoration. All He asks is that you make a conscious choice to give up your misperceptions and ingrained beliefs about yourself and others, choose wholesome and productive behaviors and attitudes, and open your mind to the bright new realities of life available only in relationship with Him.

> Now the Lord is the Spirit, and where the Spirit of the Lord is, there is freedom. And we, who with unveiled faces all reflect the Lord's glory, are *being transformed into his likeness* with ever-increasing glory, which comes from the Lord, who is the Spirit. (2 Corinthians 3:17–18; emphasis added)

Chapter 5
Why Do You Keep Doing That?

There are probably people in your life who have annoying little habits that drive you nuts, like the guy at work who's always plucking at his facial hair, or the teenager who says "I'm like" in every sentence. Although you want to shout, "Stop it!" they would wonder what you're so upset about because they're totally oblivious to their mindless habits.

It would be difficult to go through a normal day without some habits. If you were to review a typical day in your life, you might be surprised by how many useful and productive things you do out of habit, like brushing your teeth or driving the same route to work every day. A habit is any action that you've performed so many times that you do it without even thinking about it. You really only become consciously aware of a habit when it's somehow disrupted, like when you discover that all of your underwear is in the wash, or your route to work is closed for road construction. What if you had to talk yourself through every single step to dress yourself or to back your car out of the driveway? Every action in your daily routine would become moronically tedious. Of course, if you're as inept at backing up as I am, that may not be a bad idea!

Where do habits come from? Basically, if you do something that simplifies a task or makes you feel good, you will likely do it again. If you keep doing it, and if it keeps making you feel good, it will probably become a habit. Once it has become important to you, you will miss it if it is taken away. You've become attached to it.

Some habits are formed in the belief that the action will always produce the same favorable result. Although I don't play golf, I used to enjoy watching that sport on television. I found it humorous to watch some of the rituals various players went through before striking the ball. For instance, whenever Jack Nicklaus was preparing to putt the ball, he'd set his club head down, lift it and look at the hole, set it down, and lift it and look; usually he would do this three or four times before he'd finally strike the ball. I'm guessing he had made some successful putts in the past by slowing down and being more intentional with his stroke. Because that apparently worked for him before, he probably began enacting that little ritual each time he stepped up to putt in the hope of getting the same results. Over many years of playing the game, that behavior became an ingrained habit that he likely was no longer aware of. I was certainly aware of it because it began to annoy me. "Just hit the ball, Jack!"

There are some habits that you give more thought to and are more deliberate about, like making sure the doors are locked before you go to bed at night, or double-checking to be sure you've turned off the oven or the space heater. These habits are often developed for safety reasons. There are other habits that begin as the result of a stupid mistake that created some inconvenience.

While on vacation in northern Minnesota, I went into a grocery store to purchase a few items. It was only when I returned to my car that I discovered I had locked my car keys in the trunk! Although the local AAA was able to come and rescue this "damsel in distress," I vowed I would never make that mistake again. Now I make doubly sure that my keys are either in my hand or in my pocket before I close the car door or the trunk. Is it an annoyance? Sometimes. Is it reassuring? Always!

Deep wounds from the past may have caused you to build an unhealthy system of coping, and these behaviors have become ingrained and habitual because the results usually make you feel better. Pumping yourself full of caffeine might boost your productivity for a while and carry you through that important project at work, but if you go without it for a few hours, you will pay for it with a horrendous headache that only more caffeine will remedy. Nibbling on chocolate might relieve some tension and increase your energy for a couple of hours, but you may begin the battle with weight gain. Calling someone every day to talk about a problem might provide the attention you crave, but your persistent calling may become so annoying that your friend will stop answering your calls.

To change a habit, you need to turn off your automatic feelings, flip that two-sided coin we talked about earlier to reactivate your brain, and choose a wiser and healthier action.

- If your snacking has become an unconscious habit that provides a false sense of comfort, ask yourself what you really need. Are you substituting snack food for interaction with your teenager because of the tension between you? Are you mindlessly munching when you're lonely because you're afraid that a call to your friend will result in a painful rejection?
- If you overreact to some careless maneuver by another driver on the highway by yelling, gesturing, or honking your horn, ask yourself why it upset you so much. Do you think that person is actually stupid? Maybe he just made a mistake because he was late for an appointment. Do you think you're a better driver than he is? Maybe you are, but maybe he was distracted by his aging mother's nervousness about going to the doctor.

Changing habits can be simple, but simple doesn't necessarily mean easy. I've read that it takes twenty-one days to break an old habit and sixty-five days to establish a new one. In the meantime, you morph into a nervous Nellie because things aren't going your way and you're not getting your usual pleasure fix. You formed those habits in the first place because they filled a need. If for some reason the habit is stopped or taken away, the resulting craving can put you on the edge of addiction.

Habit or Addiction

There's a fine line between a habit and an addiction. A habit is something that's become part of a person's routine, like nibbling on M&M's every afternoon at work. Addiction, on the other hand, is a behavior or a craving that seems to control a person. The word *addiction* usually evokes the image of dependence on drugs or alcohol because those are such publicly acknowledged issues. However, these aren't the only types of addictions. Simply substitute the word *behavior* for *substance*, and the range of addictions increases dramatically.

In his book *Healing Life's Hidden Addictions*,[25] Dr. Archibald D. Hart states that addictions fall into two major categories: substance addictions and process addictions.[26]

- **Substance:** You can become attached to an external substance such as drugs, alcohol, nicotine, caffeine, and certain foods.
- **Process:** You can become attached to a system of behaviors like hoarding, playing video games, surfing the internet, gambling, shopping, or extreme sports like mountain climbing or cliff jumping.

What grabbed my attention was Dr. Hart's inclusion of codependent attachments to certain relationships in his list of process addictions. Having lunch with a good friend every month isn't so much a habit as it is an established routine to maintain and strengthen the relationship. However, in some cases, the desire to be with that person can become so intense that it becomes addicting. You then become clingy, requesting more and more time with your friend because you receive that sense of belonging, approval, and support that you're craving.

You can become dependent on people or activities just as easily as you can become dependent on sugar or caffeine, because they energize you. Although these dependencies don't necessarily become full-blown addictions, you can unknowingly cross that line into addiction if they begin to require more and more of your time, money, and thoughts.

A craving is a strong desire for something; an addiction is the inability to stop yourself from attaining that desire. A craving becomes an addiction when you can no longer control your response to it.

The Addictive Cycle

One complicating factor to addiction is the buildup of tolerance. Over time, the addictive behavior becomes less effective at satisfying a particular need or blocking the feelings you want to avoid. You have to ingest the substance or practice the behavior again and again, more and more often, to achieve the desired effect.

You may despise that thing you want, but your craving drives you to go after it anyway. You may make a valiant effort to not do that thing you know isn't good for you, but unless you have something healthy to replace that distorted need, your resolution will only last for as long as you can stand the craving.

Your subconscious knows exactly what you need. Unfortunately, your conscious mind can only guess, especially when you've been dragged into the darkness of depression where it's difficult, if not impossible, to muster up any kind of rational thought. All you can think of is to engage in some activity that will make you feel better about yourself, or run to that one relationship where you can hide from the intimidating world around you. Your mind is adept at creating clever new ways to manipulate people into focusing on and caring for you.

As a young adult, I had stopped maturing emotionally and had difficulty learning healthier ways to meet my need for relationship. I eventually figured out that "having a problem" generated the attention and comfort I was looking for from the people to whom I was drawn. Obviously, depression is a problem, so I started there. Sadly, I stayed there year after year because I didn't know any other way to secure the comfort, affection, and deep connection I craved.

Most of the people to whom I attached myself were those who could be defined as caretakers: a pastor, a teacher, a close friend, a therapist—anyone who showed a genuine interest in me, encouraged me, made me laugh, and taught me about life. Even though I didn't recognize what specifically I was receiving from those people, I knew it felt good and gave me a satisfying sense of caring attention and acceptance.

My depression brought me—or in the case of therapists, bought me—the caring and intimacy I was missing. As a result, the therapy went on and on ... and on and on. I couldn't end it because I had nothing to replace it with. I survived emotionally on professional friends rather than social friends.

Lesson #3 in Brain Chemistry

When you're trying to find answers, or excuses, for what's "wrong" with you and why you do what you do, you can always say, *My brain made me do it.* After all, there is some truth to that! Better yet, you can begin to understand and acknowledge that the God who created your wondrously complex brain also designed you with the ability to think and reason. You're not at the mercy of your brain chemistry. Science has shown that by making different choices and acting on those choices, you can actually reroute your brain's pathways.

Scientists have discovered that one of the most highly developed pathways in our brains is the pleasure pathway, and the primary transmitter is dopamine, one of the "feel good" chemicals. Each time we participate in an activity that releases those pleasure chemicals, providing a sense of euphoria or well-being, we get hooked on them. However, to maintain that sense of euphoria, we have to continue ingesting the substance or engaging in the behavior more often and in increasing amounts. That's because other parts of our brains play a prominent role in regulating many aspects of emotional learning and behavior. The amygdala[27] in particular is designed by our amazing Creator to step in and protect the central nervous system from overdosing on any one chemical. It does this by reducing the number of neuroreceptors. With fewer neuroreceptors to receive the repetitive message, the pleasure effect decreases, and it takes even more of the substance or behavior to maintain the same "feel good" level.

In order to feel the same level of pleasure as before, we must gamble more, consume more drugs or alcohol, spend more time on our cell phones or video games, engage in more thrill-seeking activities, acquire more things through shopping or hoarding, or increase the intensity or the frequency of our clinging or compulsive behaviors. This actually causes the brain to rewire itself so it can continue generating those dopamine highs. Thus, the cycle goes on and on, and we've unknowingly moved into addiction.

Obsessive-Compulsive Disorder (OCD)

When we think of OCD, we tend to associate it more with behaviors like repeated hand-washing, counting, checking, or following a strict routine, like opening and closing a door three times before entering. OCD is often the subject of humor or horror. We laugh at TV characters like Adrian Monk who are afraid to shake hands or touch anything without having a Wet-Wipe handy, or who have to make sure all of the glasses in the cupboard are spaced exactly the same distance apart. Then there are the serial criminals depicted in movies and on TV who horrify the world with their twisted, murderous, repetitive behaviors.

Although we might do certain things over and over again, our actions aren't necessarily compulsive. For example, in preparing for a performance, a musician may rehearse a certain difficult passage multiple times to master it and feel confident. A piano teacher in college insisted that I practice scales in different keys. He instructed me to play three octaves (series of eight notes) with both hands. Each time I made a mistake, I had to start over until all three octaves were played perfectly! In that case, the stopping and replaying was a teaching tool I followed at the insistence of a perfectionist teacher. It was called practice, not compulsion. I can assure you that I did not become obsessed with playing all scales to perfection! I still dislike playing scales even though I understand the reason for the exercise.

OCD is characterized by unreasonable and seemingly uncontrollable thoughts and fears (the obsessions) which lead to repetitive behaviors (the compulsions). Obsessions create the discomfort while compulsions attempt to reduce it. Compulsions can be mental or physical. Physical compulsions consist of repetitive behaviors such as cleaning, arranging things in order, checking, and hoarding. Mental compulsions include behaviors such as seeking constant reassurance.[28]

OCD is different from addiction in one important aspect. People who are addicted to a substance or behavior usually experience at least some pleasure in their activity. On the other hand, OCD sufferers are tormented by their obsessive thoughts to the point that they are driven to repeat their compulsive tasks even when they don't want to. They know their compulsions are irrational, but they keep doing them knowing they will provide some temporary relief from their persistent thoughts and fears.

Addicted to People

If you had asked me twenty years ago if I had ever engaged in addictive behavior, I would have said no without hesitation. However, I'm no longer able to make that declaration, and it humbles me to admit that. I had never identified a particular behavior in my life as an addiction because it was so intertwined with and buried in the darkness of my depressive thoughts and behaviors.

My own desperate search for attention, acceptance, and connection regularly found its solution in the offices of pastors and therapists. I would often make up things I needed to talk about in order to have an excuse to enter a one-on-one conversation with the pastor whose depth of thought and wisdom I admired, or the therapist who would focus on and listen to only me. I didn't even care if my problem was solvable. All I wanted was to be listened to, and I was willing to pay the therapist's fee to get that. I became addicted to therapy because for one hour, I had the undivided attention of that one person. Because I was already addicted to the process and often became quite fond of the person, I didn't want the therapy to end! It was never about getting better. It was all about getting what I needed and most longed for: deep connection and pleasant companionship.

Because of my history of feeling unloved and unwanted, I became emotionally attached to this person and was terribly frightened that this object of my need and attention would abandon me (obsessive thoughts). To reassure myself that I wasn't being ignored, I began finding more ways to be in communication with, or at least within sight of, this person on a regular basis (compulsive behavior). If for some reason I didn't find her in a place where I expected her to be, or if she didn't return my phone calls as quickly as I expected, I would become anxious and fearful. I would have such difficulty coping that I would finally have to call or email her just to reassure myself that she hadn't left my world.

The Scapegoat

The Lord made me acutely aware of this behavior one Sunday morning. The sermon that day was about the Old Testament ceremony of annual atonement for sins (Leviticus 16). One unblemished goat was killed as a sacrifice. A second goat, the "scapegoat," was used to ritually remove the burden of sin from the people. The high priest would place his hands on the goat's head, symbolically placing all of the sins of the people on the goat. The goat would then be led into the desert and released, never to be seen again, thus paying the annual price for taking away the nation's sins.

In our culture, we don't hear the word *sin* much anymore, even in some of our churches. When we do hear the word, we immediately think of murder, rape, abuse, kidnapping, theft—actions we would never think of doing ourselves. The only personal sins I could think of that day in church were little white lies or an occasional angry outburst.

That Sunday morning, a live goat was led onto the stage. Pastor Anderson then instructed the congregation to prayerfully write on the piece of paper that had been placed in their bulletins the name of their private sin. He explained, "Sin is anything or anyone that comes between us and God." In other words, whatever occupies our minds the most becomes our god. Obsessions or addictions certainly fall into that category because they consume our minds, infect our behavior, and quench our spirit.

Jesus' familiar voice in my head directed me to write down the word *idolatry*. I swallowed hard and hid my paper in shame as I wrote down that horrifying word. I was heartbroken to realize Jesus had spoken the stark truth to my heart. Me? An idolater?

Those notes were gathered up by the ushers, taken to the front, and reverently placed by Pastor Anderson into bags hanging over the goat's back. We were then able to watch on video as the goat was led out the door, down the hallway, outside, and over the hill, out of sight. It was a moving demonstration of our sins being taken away. In those moments, there were tears in my eyes as I realized that was exactly what Jesus had already done for me. "He carried [my] sins far away."[29]

In Isaiah 43:25, the Lord says, "I, even I, am he who blots out your transgressions, for my own sake, and remembers your sins no more." And in Micah 7:19 we read these words: "You will again have compassion on us; you will tread our sins underfoot and hurl all our iniquities into the depths of the sea."

It's one thing to acknowledge the truth of our sins and understand the great sacrifice Jesus made to carry them all away. But what are we to do about the obsessive thoughts and fears that are still painfully present in our earthbound minds? The Ten Commandments contain these words direct from the Lord's mouth.

> You must not have any other gods except me. You must not make for yourselves an idol that looks like anything in the sky above or on the earth below or in the water below the land. You must not worship or serve any idol, *because I, the Lord your God, am a jealous God.* (Exodus 20:3–5 NCV; emphasis added)

We have a jealous God who doesn't want anything or anyone to stand between us and His love and grace. As I struggled to force out the obsessive thoughts and fears that still ruled my mind, I began to deliberately think about Jesus as a jealous lover. I took several Post-it® notes, and I wrote two letters on each one: "JJ" standing for "Jesus is jealous." I stuck those notes all over the place: on the bathroom mirror, on the headboard of my bed, on the dashboard of my car, on the refrigerator, on my desk at work—anyplace where I would be forced to see it and think about it many times a day. Each time I found my obsessive thoughts or fears overwhelming my mind, I would quickly repeat to myself, "JJ." Faithfully He would come to me and quietly remind me that "God's peace, which is so great we cannot understand it, will keep your hearts and minds in Christ Jesus" (Philippians 4:7 NCV).

Although I still struggle from time to time with my obsessive thoughts and fears of being ignored or abandoned, it's become much easier to replace those thoughts with the image of Jesus holding me in His strong arms, lovingly tending to my need for quality time, approval, and deep connection. He continues to remind me in His Word and in my daily life that He will provide exactly what I need and will never leave me or forsake me.

Be Honest about Your Habits and Addictions

Once you've identified and acknowledged your addiction as a problem, it is no longer just a finely tuned habit that requires no thought. Now you can no longer engage in that behavior without counting the cost.

- Are you obsessing about the behavior more often?
- Are you trying to convince yourself the behavior isn't really a big deal?
- Do you organize more and more of your life so that you can engage in the behavior?
- Do you often feel guilty or ashamed of the behavior and yet find that you are unable to stop?
- Do you give yourself a pass, telling yourself that you really could quit if you wanted to?

Start now to evaluate one of the habits or addictions you would especially like to change or eliminate, and start recognizing that you *can* eliminate your addictive behavior.

- Name the habit or addiction and acknowledge that it's become a problem.
- Identify the painful emotions that lead to the habitual behavior. Is there a feeling of rejection, or failure, or desire, or fear?
- Identify the triggers that stimulate your addictive behavior. Is it a certain sound or smell? A critical remark? A need to "fix" it for everyone? Is it a way to escape some responsibility or situation that frightens you? Is it a feeling of aloneness or unworthiness?

Make a deliberate choice to eliminate the behavior by asking yourself these questions.

- Why would I want to continue this behavior? What benefit am I receiving from the behavior?
- What is the cost of continuing this behavior? What am I losing by exercising this behavior?
- Would the healthy results of stopping the behavior outweigh the benefits of continuing?
- Plan ways to avoid or defuse the trigger. Use mental or visual reminders like my "JJ" notes, or impose upon yourself some type of consequence or reward for your behavior.

Identify Your Needs

As you begin to break old patterns of behavior, you will still have needs that must be satisfied. Unrecognized and unsatisfied needs demand your attention and energy. When your needs aren't met, you can become driven to get them satisfied by any means possible, healthy or unhealthy. That's why your habits and addictions can be so difficult to break: you haven't identified the needs that trigger them. Instead of asking, "Why can't I fix this problem?" it would be better to ask, "What do I really need?"

Categories of Needs

All of our needs fall into three basic categories: physical, emotional, and spiritual. All of our behaviors, including habits and addictions, are simply an attempt to meet those basic needs.

Physical Needs

First and most basic are the needs for physical comfort and survival. We can't survive without food, water, or air. Sleep, clothing, and shelter are important for physical health and comfort. Fortunately, at least in the United States, the vast majority of people have ready access to all of these, except possibly sleep due to our varying schedules.

Emotional Needs

Most of the needs that create problems for people are in the emotional category. We generally must depend on others to meet these needs.

Problems with depression intensified in my early teenage years when I was competing with four siblings for my parents' attention. Three of my siblings are several years younger than me and my older brother, so they were the ones who, in my opinion, demanded and received the most attention and praise.

I was always trying to do anything that would garner some praise or approval from Dad. I believed I couldn't do anything good enough for him. Coming home with any grade lower than an A didn't measure up. Making a mistake during a clarinet or piano solo usually incurred a remark like, "What happened to those two notes you goofed up?" Oh, how I longed to hear something positive from Dad. Even if he did offer a compliment, I tuned it out because I couldn't believe I deserved it.

In my junior year of high school, I played a piano solo for the prom, my first solo in front of my peers. With a mixture of stage fright and excitement, I couldn't imagine the utter exposure of playing under a spotlight. Just before going on stage, I asked the light technician to shine a blue light on me rather than white—*to set the mood*, I said. After all, I was playing Debussy's "Clair de Lune" about the moon! Truthfully, I just wanted to hide in the shadows while I played.

The solo went well, and the applause from my friends was delicious. Because Dad was a high school teacher, both he and Mom were at the prom along with other faculty and their spouses. On the way home with them after the prom (that's right, I had no date!), Dad said four words I can still hear clearly to this day: "I'm proud of you." That was one sweet moment I have forever treasured. Those few words meant the world to me because they came from Dad … and because I never heard those words from him again.

Thinking back now, I believe those priceless words I longed to hear were buried deep in Dad's heart, and he simply didn't know how to express them. That was unfortunate because I eventually resorted to what would become an addictive dependence on other people to acquire those desperately needed words of praise and assurance.

The As of Need

Emotional needs tend to fall into six categories, which psychologists have labeled as the six As of need. Actually, I've added one more, so now there are seven!

Approval (Valued)

One of the biggest obstacles to improving our self-esteem is the constant need for approval by others. We believe that unless someone tells us what a great job we did or how wonderful we are, we're not good enough. Truthfully, until you believe in yourself, it will not matter what someone else says because the most important person—you—doesn't believe it.

Assurance (Security)

The most prominent of our emotional needs is for security. We must depend heavily on our external environment and relationships for these needs, which include stability, predictability, and a structured and safe environment. It's difficult to think clearly when we are unsafe or living in a continual state of fear, as do many abuse victims and people living in high crime areas.

Attention (Recognition)

Attention is the need to be noticed by other people. If we didn't receive adequate amounts of attention as a child, we might become caretakers or people pleasers to get the attention we crave. To battle feelings of insecurity or invisibility, we might spend a significant amount of energy creating situations in which we become the center of attention.

Acceptance (Connection, Sense of Belonging)

Acceptance is the need to have close relationships with individuals and to belong to groups of people who share common beliefs or goals. We all need to feel free to share our ideas, feelings, and dreams, and to feel understood and connected. We feel isolated and lonely if the group we long to be with is cliquey, or the friends we're attracted to keep secrets, are critical, jealous or selfish, engage in gossip, or are prejudiced.

Autonomy (Independence)

Autonomy is the need to be connected but separate. We need the sense of knowing how to take care of ourselves, of knowing how to think for ourselves and make our own decisions rather than having them imposed upon us by others. We need to feel free to be ourselves in any situation.

Accomplishment (Self-expression and Productivity)

One emotional need that many of us never satisfy is our need to find purpose and meaning in life; to express ourselves through our own words, actions, and abilities; and to learn something new and expand our own skills and knowledge. What holds us back from full self-expression and accomplishment? Fear of being judged. Fear of making a fool of ourselves. Fear of failure. Fear of rejection. Our core beliefs lie to us about who we are: "I'm stupid." "My ideas are insignificant." "I don't know the right people." "I'm unskilled and unfit."

Affection (Skin Hunger)

Skin hunger is the need for healthy, nurturing touch, such as a hug, a handshake, or an arm around our shoulder. Caring touch helps us feel connected to others. If we don't receive enough of this type of physical connection, we can feel isolated and emotionally distressed. Sometimes we must speak up and ask for a hug!

Take a lesson from a dog I met at a wayside stop in Alaska. Blue, a beautiful Australian blue heeler and husky mix with a gorgeous blue-gray coat and piercing blue eyes, was a happy, high-spirited animal that knew exactly what he wanted from this stranger who boldly walked over to meet him. Blue ran to me and immediately stood on his hind legs with his back pressing against me. It was obvious he was looking for a good tummy rub, and I was more than happy to oblige! When he was content with the tummy rub, he licked my face and then got on all fours and leaned toward me, receiving a pleasing back rub too!

Was I surprised by Blue's assertiveness? Not really. Unlike some people who are afraid to ask for what they need and instead play the silent game of "guess what's wrong with me," Blue simply wagged his whole body with his tail and immediately got what he wanted. He had already sensed from my behavior that I was no threat to him, so he wasn't afraid to boldly show me what he needed. The bonus was that my own skin hunger was satisfied at the same time! Give a hug; receive a hug.

Spiritual (Need for Hope)

In addition to those seven As of need, there is the spiritual need that can only be filled by connection with God. He is the one who created you with needs, and He knows better than anyone how to satisfy those needs—not just a few of them but all of them.

During a particularly difficult time when I was feeling empty and alone, Jesus spoke these words to my heart.

> Looking to other people for your needs won't fill up that hole in your heart or relieve the aching emptiness you feel. I'm the only one who can do that. But, you say, you need people? Of course, you do! I made you that way.

I've consistently brought people into your life who can provide what you need: encouragement, wise counsel, confidence, support, comfort ... and hugs. But they can't fill up all of the need I created in you. I want you to need Me more than you need them. I want to hold you while you cry. I want to show you that the pain you're running from is nothing to fear. I've brought specific people across your path who will consistently point you back to Me. I have the power to heal your pain and restore you to health. But you must choose to stop running and face your pain. Choose Me. Depend on Me. I'll always be here, and I'll always love you.

Needs Can Feel Dangerous or Scary

You have likely experienced times when your expression of need was rejected, or ridiculed, or ignored. As people disappointed or hurt you, you began to withdraw further into yourself, isolating from the very people who may have been able and willing to support and help you. You added to those thick walls that protect you and give you a feeling of safety. The new bricks in your carefully crafted walls can be made of behaviors or beliefs that are a result of the following.

Guilt	Shame	Anger	Helplessness	Confusion
Defiance	Control	Loneliness	Abandonment	Denial
Discouragement	Self-blame	Addiction	Bitterness	Busyness
Perfectionism	Isolation	Hopelessness	Frustration	People pleasing

Each brick in your wall is connected with a mortar called *pain*. Because of previous experiences with certain people who you learned were not trustworthy, you are often unable to discern who is now approachable and safe. We'll discuss the issue of safe people in a later chapter.

What Do You Need Right Now?

Eventually there may come a point when your habits or addictions become so intrusive or destructive that you will be forced to make a change. How do you even begin to change a habit or eliminate an addiction or compulsion?

You must actively interrupt the cycle of need that's driving your habitual behavior. Waiting passively for relief from your habits or addictions isn't going to work. Constantly saying "yes, but ..." and continuing in the same behavior or attitude is a good clue that you haven't found the motivation to climb out of your rut.

Have you heard the story about the little frog who got stuck in a deep rut in the road? The story has been attributed to various authors. This is one of the many variations.

> Frog was all alone in his rut. He was extremely discouraged and had stopped trying to get out. A rabbit came along in the morning and saw Frog just sitting there, looking exhausted and forlorn. The rabbit asked, "Hey Frog, what are you doing down there? You're going to get hurt if you stay there." Frog answered, "Maybe ... but I'm stuck in this rut and I can't get out." Since the rabbit was in a hurry and didn't know what to do to assist Frog in his dilemma, he just said "I'm sorry to hear that" and hopped away. Later that day, the rabbit came back the same way and was amazed to see that Frog was now sitting up on the side of the road. "Hey Frog!" the rabbit exclaimed. "How did you get up there?" Frog answered, "A Mack truck came along and I had to!"

When you feel yourself being dragged down by a destructive habit or addiction, it can be particularly helpful to look first at what you're feeling.

- Are you feeling lonely? Do you need someone to talk to? Do you need a hug?
- Are you frustrated by the demands or expectations of others? Do you need to change your yes to no in order to gain some freedom from the agendas of others?

- Are you weary and irritable and sad? Do you need some quality sleep?
- Are you fearful or confused about a change in your life circumstances? Do you need to find a friend or a mentor with whom to discuss possible options?

What one thing besides your addictive substance or action would make you feel better? Sometimes a simple conversation with a trusted friend can satisfy a whole variety of needs. Of course, God may very well send along a Mack truck to invade your rut and get you moving!

No Better Provider

There is nothing and no one other than God who can meet all of your needs perfectly and consistently. He is the only one who is never frightened by the depth of your need. Ask Jesus to provide the energy and the know-how to meet your needs in healthy, non-manipulative ways. He has all the people and resources of the world at His command.

I experienced a powerful example of this a number of years ago. As a church pianist, I played for Sunday services every week. One particular Sunday, I was extremely depressed, and the last thing I wanted to do was go to church and perform in front of a couple thousand people. But I was a chronic people pleaser and knew I was expected to be there. The church was a twenty-minute drive from my home. I cried the whole way. I had no idea what I really needed; I just knew it would feel good to have someone hold me and let me cry. Because I didn't know how to ask for something so personal, I simply told Jesus. As I stood by the worship center door and waited for the service to begin, I wanted to crawl in a hole.

But Jesus had a better idea! Seemingly out of nowhere, a friend I hadn't seen in several months appeared at the end of the hallway. She marched right up to me, wrapped her arms around me and, without a word, held on for a full minute. I knew without question that Jesus was holding me! No words were exchanged, and my need was never verbally expressed to my friend. Jesus made sure I received that long, lingering hug from a friend who was receptive to His leading.

Jesus is always available to provide for all of your needs and to guide you and teach you His Truth. If you're a child of the King, He has already sent your sins over the hill and out of sight and freed you from bondage to your destructive habits and addictions, your compulsive behaviors, and your obsessive thoughts. You can lift up your hands and freely give your idols to Him, knowing that He has tossed them into the depths of the sea.

Take these promises from His Word into your heart and remember that Jesus will always be there for you.

- You are of great value to God. (Luke 12:6–7)
- God cares about and is thinking of you constantly. (Psalm 139:17–18)
- He will search your heart and show you what it is you need to change. (Psalm 139:23–24; Proverbs 20:27; Romans 8:27; 1 Corinthians 2:10)
- He will lead you and guide you in life. (Nehemiah 9:19–21; Psalm 143:10; John 16:13; Psalm 119:105)
- He will correct you and convict you. (John 16:8; 1 Corinthians 4:4; Philippians 3:15)
- God will never forsake you even if everyone else has. (Psalm 9:10; Psalm 46:1–3).

Learn from my furry Alaska friend Blue and speak up! Go to God in confidence, eagerly asking for what you need. "And my God will meet all your needs according to his glorious riches in Christ Jesus" (Philippians 4:19).

Promise in the Clouds

I need someone to talk to, but no one has the time
to talk or listen to me, or soothe my tired mind.
My heart is clouded over just like the morning skies.
The early morning rainfall brings more tears to my eyes.

What pain will this new day bring? Will no one hear my cry?
I listen for a moment, but there is no reply.
Then as my eyes turn upward, I stare, and my heart pounds;
the western sky has granted my answer in the clouds!

There, just for one brief moment, through tears and falling rain,
the fragment of a rainbow sheds light upon my pain.
God said, "I know you're weary; I care and love you so.
And I'll be with you always no matter where you go.

When you feel sad and lonely, lost in uncaring crowds,
look up, My child—remember My promise in the clouds."

Chapter 6
Choice? What Choice?

When I look back at the interminable hours, days, and years I've spent living with and struggling with depression, I consider myself fortunate to have been able to keep functioning. I could be productive at a full-time job, although I wasn't necessarily friendly or sociable all the time. I was able to maintain my status as an active church musician, even though I often buried my dark mood in the piano keys. Thankfully, I was able to hold on to (even if in a clingy sort of way) some valuable relationships.

Many people with severe clinical depression seem unable to do even the most mundane things, like going out to the store to buy food. I desperately hurt for those people who struggle to get out of bed or do anything more than sleep and weep.

When you're depressed, you don't believe you have any control over your life because you view yourself as a nobody who has no rights, no worth, and certainly no choices. No wonder you feel battered and victimized by life. Because depression has already drained your energy, you tend to live by default, allowing the needs, demands, and agendas of those around you to determine the choices you make.

Even without the extra burden of depression, your life may be filled with overwhelming and often unfair demands on your time and resources. You race down the chaotic avenues of your life repeating the same old chant: *I have to, I have to, I have to.* You get dragged into activities you're not interested in, doing tasks you'd rather not do, or becoming a victim of someone's abusive or manipulative behavior because you don't believe you deserve anything better. Behind your fake smile and quiet compliance is a spirit that's broken and afraid. Satan applauds himself each time he is able to convince you that you're only a puny, powerless weakling he can lead by the nose anywhere he chooses.

Stop the Blame Game

Listen up! You're not powerless. You don't have to do what the world around you expects or demands of you! It doesn't make any difference what your choices have been in the past. You don't live in the past! If you want to change your choices, you can. If the choices made last week aren't working, you can always make a different choice today and get a different outcome. No choice is carved in stone. There are always other options!

"What options?" you ask. "I have to work, I have to take my kids to their after-school activities; I have to take care of my mother, who's homebound; I have to bake cookies for the kids' youth event at church; I have to take the car to the shop; I have to provide this, I have to search for that. I have to do everything!"

If you are making certain choices because you believe you have to, then you're not making a conscious choice based on where you want to be. Even if your current circumstances and ways of thinking seem to be overriding your freedom to change, you can learn to recognize and choose options that suit you better. You aren't merely a puppet on a string who must always do what your puppet master, or your spouse, or those church basement ladies, or "she who must be obeyed" (a la Rumpole[30]) tells you to do. You and only you are responsible and accountable for every decision you make.

You can't blame others for the consequences of your choices. You can't excuse your unwillingness to make necessary changes by saying, "I've always done it this way." You can't say with any certainty that nothing ever changes. The circumstances of your life will change once you (1) acknowledge the truth that where you are now is a direct result of your choices, and (2) start believing that you can make different choices to bring more satisfying outcomes.

What Are Your Choices?

You will make billions of choices in your lifetime and each choice, no matter how insignificant it may seem, affects something about you: what you do, how you spend your time, how you think, how you feel, what works for you and what doesn't.

Many of your choices come at you quickly several times a day and are so routine that you barely give them any thought, like when and what to eat, what time to get up, or what to wear. Most of your choices fit into one of three categories: choices of action, choices of attitude, and choices of emotion.

Choices of Action

The choices in this short list involve your actions.

How often you exercise	How late you stay up
How fast you drive	How you use credit cards
Paying the bills	Selecting a new car
Inviting new friends for dinner	Choosing a college major
Helping someone with car trouble	Donating to a charity

Some action choices require a bit of thought because they can stretch your financial resources, drain your mental or emotional energy, or significantly strain important relationships.

- If you're a mom or dad with children, many demands are placed on your time, energy, patience, and finances. How do you make those hard choices? Dad, how do you decide whether to play golf with the guys or go to your son's baseball game? Mom, how do you decide whether to participate in that women's Bible study or stay home and help your daughter with her homework?
- If you're trying to hold down a job so you can pay the multiple bills that fill up your mailbox, your boss requires a certain amount of time, energy, and skill to get the job done. However, if your workplace becomes an oppressive or antagonistic environment,

how do you decide if you will hold onto the security of the current job or search for another one?

- If you're a homeowner, even your house and property make certain demands on your time, energy, and resources to keep it functioning and in good repair. No matter where on your property you stand, you're always facing something that needs to be done. How do you decide whether to invest in new windows for the house or put that money into your kids' college fund?

Choices of Attitude

The choices available to you involving your attitude may seem a bit elusive because attitude is rarely thought of as a choice. You tend to believe that choices are only about the things you do or the people with whom you socialize. Choices regarding attitude can involve some difficult emotions, like frustration, or bitterness, or boredom which critically affect the outcome. Below are just a few of those choices.

- How well you listen to others
- How you handle issues at work
- How you deal with visiting a certain relative
- How often you criticize or are judgmental
- How you react to a traffic jam
- How you respond to a nosy, or a noisy, neighbor
- How you handle an unwelcome intrusion on your time

In emotionally charged situations, it's easy to give in to a knee-jerk reaction like honking your horn, yelling at the repairman, storming out of the office, or sending a nasty email. No one can force you to be in a bad mood no matter the circumstances. Allowing your volatile, supercharged emotions to control your reactions can prevent you from thinking through things logically and presenting a calm, rational attitude.

You can't choose your feelings because they are generated automatically. However, you can choose how you *respond* to those feelings, like my choice of a GrinAct to defuse an escalation of annoyance or anger.

The apostle Paul encourages us to develop a new attitude.

You were taught, with regard to your former way of life, to put off your old self, which is being corrupted by its deceitful desires; to be made new in the *attitude of your minds*, and to put on the new self, created to be like God in true righteousness and holiness. (Ephesians 4:22–24; emphasis added)

Choices of Emotion

How many times have you made a decision based on the emotions of the moment? If you're like most people, I'd guess you've made too many, and you've likely found the results to be less than pleasing. It's important to recognize the most common emotions that can prevent you from making wise choices: anger, annoyance, and insecurity or fear.

Anger

When you're angry, your thinking can become irrational and overly dramatic. You start using words like *always* and *never* to explain your frustration with a person or situation. You want things to go your way. When you don't get the results you've demanded or expected, you become frustrated. Your frustration can quickly escalate into rage if you're not aware of what you're thinking. If you jump to conclusions that are wrong, this exacerbates the problem.

Anger is a serious emotion, but just like other emotions, it can be managed if you stop and think before you speak or act. If you become furious every time you walk by your child's messy room, simply close the door! When you've calmed down, gently remind your child that you expect him to keep his personal space relatively clean and semi-organized. You might even offer a reward if he will do that consistently for a week. Discharge the anger and apply a challenge—to your child and to yourself!

Annoyance

One bad choice you often make when you're annoyed or frustrated is to complain. Yes, complaining is a choice! You know it doesn't solve anything, but you do it anyway. If you spend no more than fifteen minutes a day complaining about those people, rules, or inconveniences that annoy you, those few minutes will add up to more than five thousand irreplaceable minutes of intolerant thinking in just one year. Complaining is a waste of time! It puts the problem in control and shuts down your ability to be objective about the situation.

Insecurity/Fear

You may be surprised by how many things you do or avoid doing because of your insecurities or fears. You can defeat yourself by imagining the worst possible outcome to an impending action.

- What if I'm late to pick up my husband at the airport?
- What if I miss my turn and end up in Nebraska?
- What if my cruise liner gets sucked into the Bermuda Triangle?

Why do you allow yourself to imagine the worst? You may be afraid that if you try to make your own choices completely independent of others, you'll be blamed if it all goes wrong, and you'll feel foolish.

No Guarantees

Get rid of that "what if" kind of thinking! Making decisions can be difficult for anyone, and you may not be able to control the outcome of your choice, particularly when it involves other people. There are no guarantees in decision making. You must weigh the pros and cons, listen to your intuition, and do the best you can. Once you accept your freedom to choose and learn to believe in your ability to choose, circumstances will no longer have the power or your permission to control you.

Below are a few of the most common thoughts that can paralyze the choice-making process.

- **By not making a choice, I can't make a mistake.** Wrong! That's actually your first mistake. Not making a choice is still a choice!
- **There is only one right answer or one right way to do something.** Wrong! There are always options. Think outside the box.

- **My decision will upset someone.** Perhaps, but you're not responsible for everyone's happiness. It's *their* responsibility to choose how they will react or respond to the decisions of others.
- **If I make a bad decision, I'll have to live with it.** Maybe briefly, but you can always rethink the problem and make a different decision to gain a more satisfying result.

In the end, there's no such thing as a bad decision. You can accept the result of your choice as a lesson to be learned about what doesn't work for you. Once you've thought through and understood what went wrong, you can find other options that do work for you.

- Recognize at a conscious level why you would like to make a different choice in a particular situation. Do you need to rid your schedule of certain unwanted commitments? Do you want to make time for a new walking routine? Do you want to separate your actions from the demands of others?
- If there is more than one option to choose from, consider each one carefully and then ask yourself which option you feel most strongly about. If relationships will be impacted by your choice, it's important to consider the individuals involved as well as the benefit or loss to yourself.
- Instead of looking for the perfect choice, select the best solution for the situation.
- Once your choice is made, decide when and how you will follow through. Sooner is better! Don't delay by making excuses.
- If your choice involves what seems like a daunting task, break it up into smaller pieces and reward yourself as you complete each phase of the task. How you reward yourself is your choice!

Core Values First, Then Priorities, Then Choices

To make any choice wisely, you need to be familiar with your core values[31] and establish your own priorities. Of course, if you don't care about the consequences or outcome of your choices, then values and priorities are irrelevant. That's what Satan and his minions want you to believe so they can create even more havoc not only in your life but also in the lives of those who are influenced by your absent-minded choices.

Why Are Core Values Important?

As discussed in chapter 2, core values are the fundamental beliefs you initially learned from your parents, friends, and culture. Your values are unique to you and help to define who you are and who you want to be, so it's important to recognize these values and make appropriate adjustments to fit your specific needs and intentions. Personal core values

- highlight what you stand for;
- provide a code of conduct;
- help you understand your needs better; and
- act as an inner compass to guide your choices, intentions, attitudes, and behaviors.

Well-defined core values help you avoid making decisions that work against who you want to be. If you want the direction of your life to be guided by your choices rather than by the demands of others, it's vital to be aware of these values as you ponder your many options in life.

In the short list of core values below, there are likely at least a few words that will resonate with your sense of self. When I read the word *dependability*, I automatically think, "Yes! That's me: dependable."

Accountability	Accuracy	Ambition	Assertiveness
Cheerfulness	Clear-mindedness	Commitment	Compassion
Consistency	Contentment	Control	Cooperation
Courtesy	Creativity	Curiosity	Decisiveness
Dependability	Determination	Discretion	Efficiency
Excellence	Fairness	Focus	Generosity
Honesty	Independence	Intelligence	Loyalty
Obedience	Openness	Practicality	Self-control
Self-reliance	Sensitivity	Service	Simplicity
Speed	Spontaneity	Stability	Strength

Success	Tolerance	Traditionalism	Trustworthiness
Truth-seeking	Uniqueness	Unity	Usefulness

Look through the list above and jot down four or five of the values that resonate with you, that fill you with a feeling of purpose. Then determine if one value is more you than another. Resist holding onto words that only resemble what you've been coached to be, words that have never felt true for you. Ask yourself the following.

- Does this define me?
- Is this who I am at my best?
- Is this a filter I use to make hard decisions?

If you find yourself in a situation where you can only satisfy one of two values that define you, which one would take priority? For example, if your boss tells you to do something that you believe is irrational and a waste of time, would your decision lean toward your sense of obedience or your inner practicality? Your tolerance or your assertiveness?

Setting Priorities

When you are depressed, you generally don't think about priorities. On an average day, you tend to react like a bumper car being shoved from one task to the next without any sense of engagement or control. If your preferred activities are always taking a back seat to the agendas assigned to you by others, you'll probably feel out of balance and will be dragged down by frustration or anger. You may feel imprisoned by the shoulds in your life, and you'll allow situations, emotions, circumstances, or other people to control you. That's when you will find yourself living on the edge of "shoulda, woulda, coulda."

It's difficult to make good choices without first establishing some priorities to keep you on task and moving forward. Setting clear priorities will make it easier to

- eliminate unnecessary things from your to-do list,
- extract yourself from a current, uncomfortable commitment, and

- be more discerning when considering new demands on your time and energy.

Saying yes to one priority means saying no to other conflicting demands on your attention and time, even pleasant ones. If saying yes to someone else's need is mutually beneficial, you may certainly choose to say yes. Just be sure your yes or no is your own free choice, not a reaction to a sense of guilt or an unhealthy need to please. When considering your options, your choices will generally fit into one of the following three categories.

- Yes/No—Do it or don't do it. Do I want to look for another job? Will I agree to that volunteer opportunity at church?
- Either/Or—Choose from options. Will I spend money on all of these car repairs now, or postpone the more expensive ones so I'll have money to spend on Christmas gifts?
- Only If—Do it only if certain conditions are met. I will agree to play for that event if I don't have to be at every rehearsal.

Priorities or Goals?

A priority is an activity or need that is meaningful and vital in your life right now. Because priorities can often seem equally important, you will need to rate them from most important to least important.

A goal is an end result or experience you're planning for the future. Because you don't live in the future, it's usually more important to determine the priorities in your life that you're not willing to sacrifice before you even think about long-term goals.

To set good priorities, it helps to list some of those areas that are giving you difficulty and not getting you where you want to go. Below are some ideas to get you started. Don't set too many priorities at once! If your list of priorities is too long, you'll become overwhelmed. It may be wise to move the least important priorities to a "someday" list to focus on later.

I want to change certain behaviors, such as:
_____ stop a bad habit (smoking, drinking, overeating)
_____ overcome issues like lying, stealing, or taking unfair advantage

_____ improve self-control and eliminate procrastination

I want to have better control over my emotions, such as:

_____ anxiety, fear, tension, shyness

_____ loneliness, sadness, guilt, apathy

_____ resentment, distrust

I want to learn certain skills so I can handle problems better:

_____ social and communication skills

_____ time management, scheduling

_____ budgeting, controlling impulsive buying

I want to change the way I think:

_____ cultivate uplifting mental attitudes and self-talk

_____ be more tolerant of myself and others, accepting what is

_____ be more willing to try something different

I want to understand why I do the things I do:

_____ uncover and understand the past experiences that still bother me

_____ become aware of my self-deceptions and defense mechanisms

_____ recognize the games being played by me and by others

Making Emotional Choices

When you make an emotional choice, you need to have your priorities and values already in place so you can make calmer, wiser decisions. Several years ago, I was faced with an unwelcome emotional choice.

My dog, Muffin, was sweet and hilarious, and she loved to snuggle. I thoroughly enjoyed her for the five years she was with me. Unfortunately, just three years after I adopted her, she became deathly ill. After a few expensive visits to the vet clinic over the next year and a second frightening episode of Muffin's illness, I learned that she had an incurable disease of the intestines, which I was told was common to the breed. The disease could only be managed with a change of diet.

I always lived on a tight budget, living paycheck to paycheck like many people do. I knew I couldn't afford to throw much more money into the care of this precious pet, but I loved her and didn't want to give up on her. I knew I had to make a decision, but I wanted my choice to be wise and rational, not made in the anguished moments of her suffering. During the following months while Muffin was feeling better, I carefully thought through my options. I knew for a fact that all the expensive blood tests and medicines in the world couldn't cure her. Thus, my priorities were boiled down to either having money to live on or having a sweet dog to snuggle. After much agonizing, I made my decision: the next time Muffin's condition threatened her health and life, I would say no to any new tests, experimental medicines, or exploratory surgery. I would take her immediately to the vet for the last time, to end her suffering.

When that dreaded day arrived, I already knew what I must do. Was it heart-wrenching? Absolutely! Do I miss her playful personality and snuggles? Every day. Have I ever questioned or regretted my decision? Never, because I'd already studied my priorities and made the only choice that made sense based on my financial circumstances and Muffin's incurable condition.

A priority relates to what is happening now, in the nitty-gritty of the moment, and is defined as something or someone currently more urgent or important than another. Setting priorities early is extremely important for emotional decisions you know are coming.

What About the Situations You Can't Change?

There are multiple situations that are simply not under your control to change. There's a great example of this in an old Scottish story about two monks. There have been several variations and mutations on this story over the years, but here's a brief synopsis.

> Two monks at a monastery had worked in the fields so hard one day that they were too tired to get up the next morning for their daily prayers. The abbot of the monastery wasn't particularly pleased with them, so he instructed them to do their field work that day with peas in their shoes. Ouch! Although this punishment was extremely painful, one of the monks never complained about the discomfort. Puzzled, his friend asked, "How can you be so happy walking on these hard, dry peas?" With a pleased grin, his friend replied, "I boiled my peas."

Lesson of the Peas

Each time you make a choice, you're deciding to live actively rather than by default. In uncontrollable situations, such as a traffic accident on the way to an important meeting or an absurd workplace demand like walking on peas all day, the choice of how you approach and deal with the situation is up to you. You can use each difficulty as an opportunity to do some imaginative thinking—and maybe some maturing as a child of the Great Creator!

After Muffin became ill for the third time and I made the choice to let her go, I knew that at least some of my depression was a direct result of the grief over losing my furry companion. I was aware that the grieving process would take some time. I also knew that my deep sense of loss wouldn't go on forever. Although I still miss Muffin, I've been able to overcome the daily sadness and reengage in my normal activities. I've also found a creative remedy for the occasional nostalgia that sweeps over me: I go to the home of a friend and enjoy the snuggles and kisses of her dog Sasha (a Maltese who looks just like Muffin) while escaping all of the inconvenience and expense of owning a dog!

A New Truth

No longer a prisoner of my misconceptions,
I'm no longer shackled by chains of my past.
Transformed from a life that allowed no exceptions
to new life with freedom to chart my own path.

This truth has demolished the walls that long trapped me;
an unwilling captive, my fear held me down.
Now bathed in new light with my mind finally open,
these three simple words make a beautiful sound:

"It's my choice!"

You Always Have Choices

Our Creator God made our world with choices galore and offered us the freedom to make our own decisions. In the Garden of Eden, God allowed Adam to give names to all of the animals—a daunting task for first-comers to the world! God obviously gave Adam the intelligence and courage to choose those imaginative names that have stuck for centuries.

God has also given you the freedom to make choices that will pull you out of the gloom of feeling victimized and set you on the path to becoming your own person

- with your own agendas,
- with your own set of beliefs and values,
- with your own sensitivities,
- with your own strengths and passions, and
- with Jesus' loving arms protecting and guiding you.

Tragically, the society we live in today has lost its moral compass, and the values and rules of our ancestors—and even our parents—now seem outdated, unnecessary, and perhaps a bit weird. Strong Christian values regarding wealth, sex, power, and morality are scoffed at and labeled as old-fashioned or intolerant. People are more concerned with being politically and socially correct—or as some like to say, "being on the right side of history"—than being in step with God's Truth.

The culture we live in has no strong moral values to guide us and spins the lie that we're free to do and say whatever we like.

- We have the right to cheat on tests.
- We can be disrespectful to our parents, all authority figures, and the elderly.
- We can have sex outside of marriage anytime we want.
- We don't have to worry about making a baby because we can always get rid of the baby—abortion is a choice according to our U.S. Supreme Court.
- We can slander anyone we want.
- We can be greedy and selfish.
- We can get drunk or stoned on drugs.

- We can choose any gender orientation or lifestyle that makes us feel good.
- We can become demanding and abusive to get what we want because we're entitled.

More and more Christians are being lured into the worldly way of making choices. No wonder we're confused and depressed! We've forgotten that God doesn't offer His children unlimited choices. Have you read this list of behaviors He abhors and forbids His children to participate in?

> The wrong things the sinful self does are clear: being sexually unfaithful, not being pure, taking part in sexual sins, worshiping gods, doing witchcraft, hating, making trouble, being jealous, being angry, being selfish, making people angry with each other, causing divisions among people, feeling envy, being drunk, having wild and wasteful parties, and doing other things like these. (Galatians 5:19–21 NCV)

We've believed the lie that these things are ours to choose, but many of the things we call choices God calls evil or sin. Sin is anything or anyone that separates us from relationship with Him. We've become so desensitized to the evil surrounding us that we are now calling it good. But God says: "Woe to those who call evil good and good evil, who put darkness for light and light for darkness, who put bitter for sweet and sweet for bitter" (Isaiah 5:20).

If a relationship with Jesus is to be a priority for you, suddenly your choices are made much simpler because many of the things accepted and approved by the world as "your right" are eliminated from your lists of options.

Pleasing People or Pleasing God

When you recognize you aren't a mere puppet and can make independent choices, you need to ask yourself who you're trying to please: yourself, your peers, your culture, or your God.

God sometimes makes choices for you. Sometimes He allows you to make choices which place you in situations or relationships that are uncomfortable and disheartening. What you're often not aware of is that His goal in allowing these choices is always to teach you about Himself and to show you how to trust Him more until finally there is no longer any doubt that He is trustworthy. One such choice confronted me.

When I was thirty-five years old and unmarried, God allowed me to enter a marriage with a man I'd known at an earlier time in my life. Although I'd had no contact with him in several years, I still thought I knew him. I was wrong. I had no idea Jerry was an alcoholic. Clearly, life with an alcoholic who was also abusive was not what I had anticipated. That new reality drove me deeper into depression, and God seemed far away during our first two years of marriage. Jerry hurled at me critical remarks about everything I was doing "wrong," from how I washed my hair to how I vacuumed the rug. The mental controlling and demeaning language, the physical pushing and shoving—all of these abuses diminished me. I was already confused about who I was supposed to be. I became a mere puppet on a string with no will of my own, afraid to say or do anything that would set Jerry off into another drunken fury.

Eventually the confusion, disappointment, and emotional battering brought me to my knees. "Please God, I can't hear you. Why are you letting this happen? I feel lost and forsaken. Please tell me where you are. Show me how I'm supposed to endure this madness. Teach me how to keep loving this man who is so different from the man I thought I married."

As I finally began to hear God's comforting voice and feel His encouraging presence, I experienced a new sense of peace and trust I'd not known before. I became certain that everything would turn out the way God intended. I began to draw closer to Him, crying on His shoulder when life hurt, accepting His grace when I didn't understand, and asking Him, "How much longer?" when I grew weak and weary of the struggle.

During the four and a half years that Jerry and I were married, there were many times when I didn't think I could stand any more of his verbal, emotional, or physical abuse. I thought briefly about divorce, mostly because someone who knew nothing about me asked, "Why do you stay?" The reason that staying made sense to me was that I took my marriage vows seriously, especially the part about promising "before God … to have and to hold, from this day forward, for better, for worse, for richer, for poorer, in sickness and in health, to love and to cherish, till death parts us, according to God's holy ordinance."

In those few tumultuous years of marriage, the only thing I was sure of was that God had brought Jerry and me together for a purpose. Although it wasn't long before I started questioning what that purpose could possibly be, I had chosen to trust the Lord to lead me and to always take care of me ... and so I stayed.

Disclaimer: Lest you think that I'm advocating staying in an abusive relationship, think again! Every situation in which you find yourself is highly unique and deeply personal.

- You're at a different stage of your life emotionally, financially, and spiritually.
- You feel things differently, and your emotions take you to different levels of anger, self-doubt, fear, or hopelessness.
- Your financial situations allow or prohibit certain choices.
- You may not have learned how (or are afraid) to set clear boundaries.
- There may be children who will be deeply impacted by your choices.

Even though I truly did want to honor my commitment to Jerry and to my Lord, there were other factors at play in my decision to stay in the marriage that were not especially honorable or wise or rational. I was so emotionally needy, so driven to pleasing people, and so doubtful of my worth as an independent human being that it could easily have been uncertainty and fear that kept me stuck in that marriage. Nonetheless, our wise God used those very issues and inclinations to teach me about Himself and His faithfulness, about His attention to every detail of my life, and about His continuing protection over me.

Knowing what I know now and being more confident of my value as a child of God, I might make a different choice about staying in that marriage. One thing that would play a significant role in staying or walking away was the level of physical abuse. If I ever truly feared for my life (thankfully, I never did), I would not stay. I don't believe God ever intends for any of His children to be abused just for the sake of honoring a commitment to Him. He's well aware of the impact of evil on His people, and I firmly believe that if we choose to stay close to Him and seek His guidance in all of our choices, He will either protect us or deliver us from evil.

Once I had resolved to stay in the marriage for better or for worse and to trust Jesus to keep me safe, I began to catch glimpses of His comfort and protection, as well as some inner strength I didn't know I had. One night I was lying alone in bed, completely exhausted and crying. I pleaded, *Jesus, I can't do this anymore.*

Through the sighing of the wind in the trees outside my window, I heard Him say, "One more day." Those three words, whispered in the dark hours of the night, spoke volumes to my broken heart. Matthew 6:34 (NCV) tells us not to worry about tomorrow, "because tomorrow will have its own worries." That night I chose to go through one more day, then the next, and the next … just one more day at a time, trusting that Jesus would stay close beside me.

In our fifth year of marriage, Jerry experienced serious medical problems and was hospitalized for a month. Just thirty days after he was dismissed from the hospital to be cared for at home, his body finally succumbed to all the damage done by his diabetes, his alcoholism, and the medical trauma of colon surgery. He died at four in the morning, just after the paramedics arrived. I knew immediately, without question, that the Lord had rescued me. The paramedics even commented on how calm I seemed. At that moment, I was snuggled up close to Jesus. I had chosen to trust Him implicitly to keep me safe, "for better or for worse, in sickness or in health, till death parts us." I was absolutely certain that He honored my trust in Him by relieving me of the impossible decision to stay or leave that abusive situation. Jesus made the choice for me and was there to comfort me in my grief.

Hopefully, that's not the kind of choice you will have to face in life. But with that choice, I learned quite dramatically that God is faithful, compassionate, and gracious when we choose to seek His face and honor Him even though the darkness of our pain seems to suffocate us.

> Even the darkness will not be dark to you; the night will shine like the day, for darkness is as light to you. (Psalm 139:12)

I believed it then, and I'm more convinced now, that when honoring and trusting Jesus is at the forefront of your choice-making processes, then whatever choice you make and whatever the outcome, Jesus is always able to teach you valuable lessons about trusting Him, about living Christianly through the joys and sorrows of this life, and about how precious you are in His sight. In your most difficult moments, He will surprise you with His mercy, draw you into His sanctuary of peace, and lavish His soothing love all over your weary soul.

Once you've made the ultimate decision to make pleasing Jesus a priority, defining and developing your values becomes less problematic or fearful.

> And whatever you do, whether in word or deed, do it all
> in the name of the Lord Jesus, giving thanks to God the
> Father through him. (Colossians 3:17)

Today, the Lord continues to speak lovingly to me through my favorite verse about choices.

> I have set before you life and death, blessings and curses.
> Now choose life, so that you and your children may live
> and that you may love the Lord your God, listen to His
> voice, and hold fast to Him. *For the Lord is your life.*
> (Deuteronomy 30:19-20; emphasis added)

Choice

Choice. It's not a big word,
but it's opened up the door
to this life-changing view:
I'm not a victim anymore.
Freed from "poor-me-itis"
and a chronic need to please,
I've learned that choosing truth
instead of lies can bring real peace.

Jesus' love pursued me
and released me from my shame.
He set me free to hear His truth.
Just one more thing remained:
"You don't need to know
why you've been hurting all these years."
He whispered, "I can heal your wounds
and dry up all your tears."

As He held me close, He said that I could trust His grace.
When I hesitated, a bright smile lit up His face.
He winked and said, "I'll take your pain
and free you to rejoice.
But I won't force your trust in me.
Guess what? You have a choice!"

Chapter 7
Who's in Charge?

An early morning phone call from a friend woke me up one Saturday. She was excited about a picnic she'd planned with her girls for the day and informed me that she would pick me up at 10:30. She didn't ask me if I had other plans or even if I wanted to go. She just assumed I would—and she was right. I did go, but only because I believed I hadn't been given a choice. Needless to say, I resented every minute of the picnic time because I knew I'd been manipulated into going when I had other things I'd rather be doing—like sleeping in!

Because I believed I had to please people to make them like me, I did what my friend said and was ultimately stuck with my frustration. Fortunately, it didn't take me long to realize that I was the one who had actually made the choice to go. I recognized that I could make a different choice if faced with similar circumstances in the future. The next time I was confronted with either being manipulated by my friend or controlling my own agenda, I was able to say, "Sorry, I have other plans." What a liberating moment!

Although I don't have any statistics to confirm my belief, I can say with some certainty that the majority of the problems we encounter in life are those involving other people. I daresay life would be much less stressful without bosses, siblings, teachers, customers, or politicians! Yet it's the variety of people in our lives from whom we learn much about relationship, and about ourselves.

The important people in our lives often have something we need, such as attention, approval, and comfort, so we tend to believe we must follow their agendas in order to maintain the relationship. Depending on how highly we value their roles in our lives, we become willing to do or say almost anything to satisfy them, tagging along like a lost puppy.

Bending to the demands and expectations of others too often results in giving up who we really are. When we depend on the perspective of others to define our identity, we draw our sense of self-worth and our beliefs from them. In doing so, we surrender our independence, our self-respect, and our integrity. We may even endure physical or emotional abuse just to maintain the relationship.

When we look outside ourselves for self-definition, we relinquish our power and set ourselves up to be victims. We become more and more frustrated and disappointed with life as we struggle to set our own direction.

What Is a Boundary?

What do you immediately think of when you hear the word *boundary*? Something you're not allowed to do? Some place you're not supposed to go? *Merriam-Webster's Dictionary*[32] defines a boundary as "something that indicates or fixes a limit or extent." Another definition is "a point or limit that indicates where two things become different" (such as ideas, rules of behavior, beliefs, and attitudes).

A boundary is a property line. It defines where your property ends and where someone else's begins. Think of it as a house with many rooms. You are the owner and get to decide who you let in and who you keep out, who is allowed access to all of the rooms, and who is limited to the living room.

People who try to invade your space aren't thinking about you or how pushing the limits of your boundaries will affect you. They may even think they're entitled to get whatever they ask for, believing their needs and demands are more important or more urgent than yours. To protect your boundaries, you must know and respect your own needs and beliefs in order to resist being pressured or bullied into a course of action that is unacceptable or uncomfortable for you.

The more manipulated you think you are, the more likely you are to continue building your "Fine" walls to hide your true feelings. When a relationship starts to crumble and the other person asks, "What's wrong?" your rote response is often, "Nothing, I'm fine." In these cases, your Fine mantra becomes "Feeling Indignant, Nameless, and Exploited."

People who have walls instead of boundaries may have been deeply hurt by others and have erected barriers to prevent being hurt again. Although walls may protect you from the real or imagined impositions of others, they also prevent you from building trusting, caring relationships.

The definitions of boundaries and barriers clearly show the differences.

- A boundary is a dividing line that marks the limits of an area; a barrier is a fence or obstacle that prevents movement or access.
- A boundary provides room to move around with protection readily available; a barrier imprisons you and keeps you isolated from people.
- A boundary is like a fence with a gate that can only be opened from the inside; a barrier is like a heavy shield you drag around with you.
- When you establish a personal boundary, you're asserting your right to pursue your agendas, to own your needs, and to think and choose independently; when you use barriers to hide behind, you're constantly on guard against intrusions.[33]

The difficulty with setting boundaries is that they might offend someone. Although you can't set limits on what other people do or how they react, you can draw some lines between what you will or will not tolerate. You can also limit your exposure to those people who are unwilling to respect your boundaries.

Genesis 3 reveals that God allowed Adam and Eve and all humankind to be whoever they chose to be, yet He set standards and boundaries to protect them. He only separated Himself from Adam and Eve when they disrespected His standards and crossed His specific boundary: "You can be that way if you choose, but I must now evict you from this Garden because you ate the fruit from the tree of the knowledge of good and evil, which I have forbidden." (Genesis 3:22, my paraphrase)

Misperceptions about Boundaries

The following misperceptions can keep you from setting healthy boundaries in your relationships.

A boundary is a rejection. Wrong! You may be hesitant to set boundaries in your relationships for fear you'll be misunderstood or rejected. It might seem easier to just go along rather than to draw a line in the sand, but it's definitely not emotionally healthier!

Setting boundaries means I'm selfish. Wrong! In "church speak," having a servant heart is often translated to mean you're selfish if you don't eagerly give your time, talents, and resources to those who need them. You can be manipulated into believing that your own wants, needs, and priorities take a back seat to serving in the church.

Boundaries are permanent, and I'm afraid to burn my bridges. Wrong! You own your boundaries, and they are flexible and movable. If you set limits with someone, and that person responds in a healthy, mature way, you're free to renegotiate those boundaries.

Boundaries allow me to control whether people act in hurtful ways toward me. Wrong! People have their own problems and will behave accordingly. However, you can control whether you allow yourself to be impacted by the attitudes and behaviors of others.

A boundary will enable me to control whether people continue to get themselves in trouble. Wrong! You can control whether or not you will continue to bail them out. Before you agree to help, ask yourself, "Is this something they can do for themselves? Will I resent giving away my own resources (time, money, skills, etc.) if they're unwilling to accept personal responsibility for their own messes?"

It's okay to put up with some inconvenience or to sacrifice some time and resources if you value the relationship or the anticipated outcome more. However, when you put someone else's priorities ahead of your own, you lose your sense of self-worth and personal identity.

Areas That Need Boundaries

In order to exercise your right to set your own boundaries, it's important to understand what specific aspects of your life require boundaries.

Physical. You own your body, and no one has a right to touch it without your permission. You must learn to recognize and welcome the tender hug from a friend and to discourage and repel the inappropriate touch of a stranger, or even a coworker who seems to be getting too comfortable with you.

Emotional. You have a right to respectfully express your own feelings to others. You have a right to set limits on how much you will emotionally invest in your relationships. You have a right to reject emotional violations by others, such as being lied to, manipulated, bullied, or shamed.

Time, Skills, and Resources. You are in charge of your own schedule, skills, and resources, and you can decide when and how much to give to others and when to reserve it for yourself. You can choose how, when, and where to develop and share your talents and skills. You have a right to set limits on the use of your money, house, car, and other personal property.

Spiritual. You have a right to spend as much time as you want or need in the pursuit and enrichment of your relationship with God. This is the most valuable and most life-changing relationship of all. Don't allow the siren call of the world to steal it from you.

Walked On and Weighed Down

Without boundaries, you may continue to struggle with self-esteem issues. You could unknowingly become manipulative and demanding as you try to subtly control other people's connection with you in order to satisfy your emotional needs. There are both healthy and unhealthy ways of nurturing your personal needs. Being manipulative is certainly not the healthy way.

If you're on the receiving end of manipulative behavior, you might sense that something isn't quite right, but you can't clearly pin it down. If you have no boundaries, manipulators will have open license to subtly control the way you do life. This could range from how much time they expect you to spend with them, what you should or should not buy, how you ought to behave around others ... the list is endless.

With no boundaries in place, you have little or no protection against the subtle manipulations of others. This can cause you to doubt yourself and blindly react to a situation out of frustration, confusion, or anger. If you erect an arbitrary boundary based on some out-of-control emotion or unacknowledged need without considering the possible consequences, you may be faced with a whole new set of problems.

Heed the Warning Signs

Two signs that boundaries are weak or nonexistent are feelings of discomfort and resentment.

- Discomfort is an uneasy sense that something about the situation or person goes against your instincts or beliefs.
- Resentment comes from being taken advantage of or not being appreciated. It's often a sign that the expectations placed on you are inconvenient or demeaning and have pushed you beyond your limits.

Both discomfort and resentment can be the triggers that will coax you into informing or showing others how you prefer to be treated. The key is to tell the truth and assertively communicate your boundaries without being threatening.

> I will not allow others to define my mood, method, image, or mission.
>
> —Author Unknown

One of the men I worked with for a number of years was notorious for bringing work to me that he claimed must be done right away. I did my best to accommodate him, but eventually his demands became almost a daily occurrence. My own workload was enormous, and I knew for a fact that he was promising his clients that he could deliver the requested document that day, usually by noon, without asking me first whether that was even possible. I began to resent being treated like a machine that would crank out his work on command.

Instead of becoming angry, I used this opportunity to practice my freshly acquired boundary-setting skills. The next time he came to me with another urgent demand, I advised him as calmly as I could that I already had several projects on my desk that were also pressing. I offered to finish his document before I left for the day. At first he whined that he had already told his client he would have it by noon. I quietly suggested that he call his client back and tell him the truth: not possible!

After listening to his demands and manipulative whining a few more times while holding fast to my boundary, he finally began asking me *when* I could complete his document. I was usually able to squeeze his work in between larger projects and hand it to him well before the end of the day. We both learned a valuable lesson about setting healthy boundaries. Well, at least one of us did!

Boundaries aren't just a sign of a healthy relationship; they're a sign of self-respect. They're about protecting and growing the person you are. Although you have no control over how other people behave, you can set limits on the time you spend with those people with whom you feel uncomfortable or manipulated. You can set boundaries that protect your space, your time, your emotions, and your resources by adding these phrases to your vocabulary.

- No
- I disagree
- Let me think about that
- I will not
- I prefer not to
- I'll check my calendar
- I'll check with my spouse
- Stop that
- Don't touch me
- Enough

When you set limits and protect your boundaries, you'll learn a lot about the other person. When you say no to others, they may be insulted or inconvenienced because they aren't getting what they want. *That doesn't mean you're wrong.* If your new boundary upsets them, that's their problem. You are not responsible for other people's reactions to your decisions. You are only responsible for communicating and implementing your boundary in a respectful manner.

Some people, especially those accustomed to controlling, abusing, or manipulating others, might test your boundaries. Plan on it and expect it, but stand firm! You cannot successfully establish a clear boundary if you send mixed messages by apologizing or backing down. Your yes has no meaning if you never say no.

No is a complete sentence. It does not require justification or explanation.

—Anne Lamott[34]

Creating Healthy Boundaries

Once you have identified the areas of boundaries you need for healthy relationships, then you are ready to take the steps necessary to prioritize and establish those boundaries. An excellent tool that is helpful in determining and establishing priorities in any relationship is the "Priorities Worksheet" created by Marsha Linehan for her *Skills Training Manual*.[35] Below is a compilation of the main principles in that process.

Priorities in Relationships

Prompter: What about this situation makes me uncomfortable, resentful, or angry?

Possible answers:

– My rights or wishes are not being respected.
– I want/need to say no or resist pressure to do something.
– I want to eliminate an area of conflict with this person.

Possible choices:

Objectives: What specific results do I want to achieve? What changes do I want the other person to make? What changes do I need to make to manage my choice?

Relationship: How do I want the other person to feel about me once I've made my choice and expressed my limits?

Self-respect: How do I want to feel about myself once the choice has been made and expressed?

Priority: Which is more important to me in this instance? My objectives? The relationship? My self-respect?

For an example of how this can work, go back to that friend with whom I reluctantly went on a picnic. I was acutely aware that something about that relationship would have to change, at least for the sake of my emotional health.

- I knew that the relationship was no longer a priority for me. I felt emotionally drained by my friend's dominating attitudes, and I resented the ease with which she was able to manipulate my agendas and my beliefs about myself.
- I had no expectations that my friend would need to make any changes in her behavior because I was no longer interested in maintaining the relationship.
- Any changes would be my choice, not hers, and I knew that making my own choices and acting on those choices would significantly boost my self-esteem.

It didn't take me long to choose self-esteem as my priority. Regretfully, the severing of the relationship was rather abrupt. I hadn't crafted any gentle way to walk away. I simply did what I had to do. I certainly learned some difficult and painful lessons through that incident.

Once you've thought through and established your priorities in setting a particular boundary, then you need to describe what action you intend to take to implement and enforce that boundary. It isn't enough to just set boundaries. You also must be willing to do whatever it takes to protect those boundaries. With no consequences to the other person, a boundary is meaningless. This is not a choice to feel guilty about. The reason for the boundary is to free you from unwanted or uncomfortable obligations.

Important! Although setting boundaries is crucial, it is just as crucial to respect the boundaries others have set for themselves. Setting and respecting boundaries is a two-way street. Take time to think through all boundary proposals—yours and theirs. Once you've considered your options, offer a bold yet reasonable appeal as you define your own boundaries. Also, provide a well-considered, honest response to the boundary requests of others.

Communicating Your Boundaries

Once you've defined a boundary and decided how to enforce it, you need to communicate your boundary to the people who will be directly affected. Don't assume that others will automatically understand what you think, feel, and want. No one can read your mind! If you fail to describe your boundaries clearly, nothing will change. It's important to convey to others, without blaming, how their behavior or expectations are affecting you and what changes you're choosing to make.

The Awareness Wheel, developed by Sherod Miller for his book *Straight Talk*,[36] is an excellent internal processing tool that can teach you how to approach an unpleasant or dismaying conflict in a proactive manner. It's up to you to teach people how you want to be treated. Like any new skill, assertively communicating your boundaries requires practice and patience.

The Awareness Wheel avoids blaming, finger-pointing words such as "You make me so mad" or "How could you do that to me?" This tool can teach you how to start personalizing with "I" statements: I sense; I think; I feel; I want; I will. This can simplify the process of clarifying your issues and needs.

I sense—Describe the behaviors or circumstances that are causing discomfort or resentment:
"When I try to talk to you while you are watching television and I have to say your name three or four times before you respond ..."
I feel—Always use I statements to share your feelings:
"I feel angry, hurt, discounted, unimportant, insignificant, invisible."
I think—Once you've described the distressing behavior or circumstances and how you feel, it is important to clarify its impact on you and express your personal interpretation:
"When I try to talk to you while you're watching television, and I have to say your name three or four times before you respond, I feel angry, hurt, invisible, unimportant, insignificant because it seems like I'm being punished for something, or that you don't love me."
Important: Before going on, actively listen for the response and use active/reflective listening: "I hear you saying ..." Then give the person the chance to clarify if necessary.

I want—Don't be too general. Saying "I need to know I'm important to you" is not specific enough. Describe the behaviors that would provide the message you want:

"I want you to answer me when I talk to you. I want you to ask me how my day went and really listen to my answer."

I will—Be clear about the action you plan to take or the behavior you plan to change, and be willing to set consequences for not honoring your boundary:

"If you don't do this, then I will _____." Because your new boundary will have more impact on the other person than on you, it is important to be sensitive yet truthful.

As you begin making your own choices and setting personal boundaries, the transition period may be uncomfortable for you and for those who've become accustomed to the old you.

- Each situation can be seen from different points of view, so pay attention to the perspectives of the other person.
- Clearly set limits about who can or cannot come into your space and what you expect of them once they are there.
- Be open and honest about your feelings, and be willing to accept and understand the other person's feelings.
- Learn when to use humor and when to be serious.
- Do not nag, yell, whine, or argue.
- Always check to make sure others have correctly heard and understood your words and intentions.
- Don't use excuses or fall for them. Watch for those hooks that can easily manipulate you to change your no to yes and abandon your boundary. If you're uncertain, tell people you'll consider their request and get back to them with your response.

Feeling uncomfortable is a clue that you're doing something different! Don't give up, and don't give in to pressure from others to go back to the way you were.

Some piano teachers encourage their students with the phrase "Practice makes permanent."[37] The same incentive is true for setting boundaries. Establishing and maintaining new boundaries will require patient practice until the process feels natural and comfortable.

Let Go of Control

Once you've taken steps to establish boundaries, then you're ready for the hard part: giving up your unrealistic expectations and the need to control people or situations. When you set any kind of boundary, you must be willing to let go of the outcome.

It's natural to desire certain outcomes. Two people can influence each other continuously, trying to live up (or down) to each other's expectations. The story of Martha and Mary in Luke 10:38–42 is a good example of expectation and disappointment. Mary chose to sit at the feet of Jesus. Martha chose to work in the kitchen and prepare the food. Martha was disappointed because she expected Mary to help in the kitchen instead of sitting around and chatting.

Unrealistic expectations are at the root of disappointment. Instead of looking to others to meet your needs, you must take responsibility for your own life and make necessary changes that are in your best interest. Don't spend your energy trying to change your partners and friends to fit an unrealistic image of how they can provide for your needs. Untwist your thinking and behavior and follow your own path!

Do you feel like you're constantly being let down? Do you feel like nothing ever goes as planned? Are you frustrated? Do you know why? It probably has to do with your expectations. It's important to work on removing the extra, unnecessary expectations that weigh you down.

Don't lower or raise your expectations—completely eradicate them!

How?
- First, identify your expectations.
- Second, decide which expectations are unrealistic and let go of them.
- Third, learn to be curious and flexible regarding the possible responses to your boundary requests.

In her book *Rising Strong*, Brené Brown states: "Choosing to be curious is choosing to be vulnerable because it requires us to surrender to uncertainty."[38] Curiosity allows us to be open to possibilities without needing to "fix" things. Curiosity will also cause us to suspend any judgment about what might happen.

Become Proactive, Not Reactive

The difference between responding proactively and simply reacting is choice. If you find yourself reacting, step away and regain control of your thinking. When you react, others are in control; when you respond proactively, you are in control. Begin to say what you feel, what you like, what you want, what you will do, what you will choose. Also say what you don't agree with, don't like, and won't do. But be gentle and tactful!

Develop your own interests separate from the interests of those important people in your life. Begin finding ways to trust and celebrate your uniqueness in Christ.

- Trust that you will be able to discern when something isn't right.
- Trust yourself to not hide your feelings and to make sure that your needs are satisfied in healthy ways.
- Trust yourself to know that no matter what other people may think or say, you will be able to take care of yourself.
- Trust that, if a relationship is not working, you will be able to remain a wholly functioning individual.

Trust God with Your People Needs

When you learn to trust God with the uncontrollable and seemingly unchangeable people and circumstances in your life, relax and enjoy the freedom of focusing only on what you can control. When the uncontrollable people or things in your life are making you miserable, it's because you're allowing them to do that.

The apostle Paul provides this important instruction.

> Don't become so well-adjusted to your culture that you fit into it without even thinking. Instead, fix your attention on God. You'll be changed from the inside out. Readily recognize what he wants from you, and quickly respond to it. Unlike the culture around you, always dragging you down to its level of immaturity, God brings

the best out of you, develops well-formed maturity in you. (Romans 12:2 MSG)

Trust God with the process of establishing and maintaining your boundaries. You'll be more productive, you won't be as weary, and you'll get along more easily with people. You will also develop a deeper connection with Jesus. The uncontrollable will become tolerable and manageable when you are focused on His Truth and covered by His grace.

Trust God's Boundaries

While reading in the Gospels about Jesus' time on earth, I noticed that there was nothing passive about His dealings with people! He set firm boundaries and wasn't always calm or gentle as evidenced in His confrontation with the money-changers in the Temple. He spoke the truth in love and said no to inappropriate behavior. He didn't always do what people wanted him to do. In many cases when He did help others, He expected them to do their part, like when He informed Moses that he and the Israelites would need to step into the Red Sea and go forward to be saved from the Egyptian soldiers who were pursuing them.[39]

What I had not yet learned about Jesus is that He will sometimes ask *me* to set a boundary in my own life that isn't especially welcome.

You've already read a bit about my busy life as a musician at a megachurch. In early 2010, I stopped publicly playing the piano. It wasn't because I suddenly quit out of anger or lack of commitment. Quite the contrary. Playing the piano will always be my God-given passion and joy.

Actually, the Lord came to me with a question straight out of the Gospel of John, chapter 21. "Bev, do you love me?"

My initial thought was, *Silly question!* But I boldly proclaimed, "Of course I love you!"

Jesus then asked again, "Bev, do you really love me?"

Slightly puzzled by His repeated question, I replied, "You know I do."

Jesus paused for what seemed like an eternity—probably for dramatic effect! Then He quietly asked, "Bev, do you love me more than you love your music?"

Oh, dear. My heart skipped a beat. Caught off guard, the retort that popped into my head was, *Can I get back to you on that?* Of course, Jesus already knew what I was thinking. I was so taken aback by His question that I could only feebly answer, "Of course I love you more. But why are you asking me this?"

Gently and quietly, He answered, "I want you to walk away from all of this and follow Me."

What? All of this? This stage? This marvelous piano? This opportunity to play such amazing music for these people? What do you mean by all of this? This choir and orchestra? This church? These friends? The tears welled up in my eyes as I envisioned a life apart from performing music.

The obvious question that escaped my tongue was, "Does this mean I won't ever play the piano again?"

Like a patient dad answering his overly imaginative child, He winked and asked, "Did you hear Me say that?"

Well, no. When I looked into His eyes and saw those oceans of love, my answer came easily. "Okay, Lord, I can do that for you."

I'm disappointed to tell you that although I did stop playing publicly, it took me more than a year to drag myself away from the choir loft where my friends were and from that church home where my heart was. Explaining my decision to the choir and the church leaders was one of the most difficult things I've ever done. Some understood and accepted my choice; others clearly didn't understand, and I felt sad. When I did leave, it was quite abruptly, without even a goodbye. I suddenly knew it was time.

I spent four months searching for another church to call home. The second church I visited touched my heart and drew me in. However, I wanted to be sure this was where Jesus wanted me to be, so I visited six other churches. None satisfied or felt more like home than the second one. I've been worshiping there now for the past eight years and have been blessed with many new friends.

I wish I could tell you that I stepped obediently and cheerfully into my new role as a backseat musician at my new church home. Guess what? This church had a small choir and a grand piano! Wanting to get acquainted with a few people right away, I showed up at the first choir rehearsal of the season with a smile on my face and hope in my heart. It wasn't long before I was sitting at the piano bench, once again enjoying my familiar role as an accompanist. My long-suffering Lord allowed me to play for the choir three times that year: Thanksgiving, Christmas, and Easter. What sheer delight!

Then, suddenly there was no choir! Various reasons were given for disbanding the choir: not enough people to cover absentees, no new recruits waiting in the wings, and scheduling conflicts. Yet I knew in my heart there was another reason: I couldn't resist the chance to play again, so Jesus quietly removed the temptation. I wasn't offended or angered by His intervention. Actually, I thought it was a cool sleight of hand! One day I was playing for this small choir and having fun. Then poof! In the twinkling of His eye, there was no more choir. Pretty clever, Lord!

What truly surprised me was that as quickly as the choir disappeared, so did my desire to play publicly. I thought of Psalm 37:4. "Take delight in the Lord, and he will give you the desires of your heart."

Taking delight in the Lord means that our hearts find true peace and fulfillment in Him. If we find our satisfaction and worth in Christ, scripture says He will give us the longings of our hearts. Does that mean if we busy ourselves at church every Sunday, God will give us a million dollars? Or a new boat? Or a quick sale on our house? Or that longed-for new baby? No. When we truly delight in the things of the Spirit, our desires will begin to parallel His, and we will never go unfulfilled.

That truth played itself out vividly as I was finally able to worship deeply in mind and in spirit. I found true worship to be impossible as a piano accompanist because my mind was always on what happens next. For awhile I was content in my new role as a worshiper. I was a good girl and didn't cross any boundaries. But I wondered why Jesus hadn't yet revealed my new direction in this church. In the book of John, He at least gave Peter a few hints!

I spent my time floundering, puzzling over why Jesus had brought me to this place. Although I was invited to join a couple of small groups where I developed closer relationships, the years dragged by without any inkling of what I was supposed to do in this musicless season of life. I sank again into depression and almost convinced myself that Jesus had sent me into the desert to abandon me.

I received multiple suggestions from my new friends on how I could be useful in this church community, but none of their suggested venues or activities had anything to do with my spiritual gifts or abilities. Some of my friends began hinting that I was uncommitted to serving in the church. The comment I heard too often was, "You should be using your talent for the Lord." It did no good to inform those people that I'd been using my talent for more than fifty years! Once more my brain began to pound out that familiar refrain: "not good enough."

God had other plans. Because I now had time to do more personal Bible study, it soon became evident that this was my task for the present. As I entered into more deliberate, intensive study of the Word, my relationship with and understanding of my Creator and Lord quickly became deeper, more relevant, and more precious. I eventually gathered up enough courage to ask Jesus once again, "What exactly is it you want me to do?"

His answer was quite simple. "I want you to live in the moment and be available to whoever or whatever I place in your path."

Much to my surprise—why am I ever surprised by Jesus?—He showed me what He meant the very next evening! At a Christmas concert at another Twin Cities church, I sat down next to strangers, a lady and her husband. As we were waiting for the concert to begin, the lady and I began to chat. She told me of her sadness at her recent loss of opportunities to keep singing at her church. She was questioning her worth as a singer and feeling useless. Talk about traveling the same road! I listened as she joined the audience in singing some Christmas carols. She had a beautiful voice! I encouraged her to keep singing and was able to share some of my story with her. When the concert ended, she turned to me and hugged me as she whispered, "I believe God put you here just for me."

Okay, lesson learned! As I began opening my eyes and spiritual ears to the people around me—at church, in the grocery store, in a parking lot—I experienced a new peace in my heart. I felt content with the Lord by my side. Of course, just when I was feeling settled in my new role of being in the moment, Jesus presented a challenge to that earlier commitment I had made to Him. He temporarily revised the boundary He had set for me!

During the pre-Easter season, one of the men at church, a Jewish believer in Christ, was preparing to present a Seder supper service on a Saturday afternoon to anyone who was interested in learning about this yearly Passover event observed by Orthodox Jews. I wasn't planning to go since I was already familiar with the tradition, having participated in other Seder services at my previous church home. Then I received a call from Marc, who was involved in planning the event. He was looking for a pianist to play for a vocal soloist and the congregational singing.

Marc already knew about my "no playing" boundary. He assured me that I was free to say no, but he pleaded with me, saying he had called every pianist in the church, and no one was available. I couldn't imagine going back on my promise to Jesus. Then something strange happened. Marc's voice faded into the background, and I heard Jesus saying, "I want you to do this in honor of my people Israel." Jesus' voice then vanished, and I could hear Marc clearly again.

I was certain the voice I heard was Jesus—Marc didn't talk like that! I quickly told Marc that I would play for the service and requested further details. Although I could have said no, I was acutely aware that to do so now would be saying no to the Redeemer of Israel and my Lord! Jesus had revised His boundary and urged me to agree to this musical opportunity. It soon occurred to me that no one else in the church was available to play because Jesus had already chosen me for the task!

Jesus does indeed have boundaries, and He showed me that boundaries can be flexible and somewhat unpredictable depending on the situation. The gate to a boundary can be opened again as quickly and as effortlessly as it was closed in order to allow for special circumstances. Curiously, since that Seder event, no other requests have come my way. At least for now, that gateway to playing the piano publicly remains closed.

Now I'm following Jesus in a new direction: writing this book! I've been hearing His voice more clearly and more often, and the many new things He's been teaching me about life and about Himself are far more satisfying than all of the public performances in the world. My passion for playing the piano is now directed upward, in the privacy of my home, with Jesus as the only audience. I'm playing only for His pleasure and mine—and it's delightfully fulfilling.

Chapter 8
What Are You Afraid Of?

One morning, I woke up before the alarm went off. I usually stay pretty still while I sleep, with very little tossing and turning. This particular morning, I woke up feeling panicked. The room seemed extremely dark. I couldn't see the light on the alarm clock, which was right beside my bed, but its loud ringing had startled me awake.

What was wrong? I had somehow gotten myself turned around in the bed so that when I woke up, I wasn't looking toward the clock. I was looking at the headboard! No wonder it was dark!

Our lives can be like that. We wake up in the middle of our chaotic lives and discover it's darker than it's supposed to be. We think the power has gone out and we panic, believing our lives are out of control.

Fear: The Four-Letter Word

Given the right conditions, every possible level of fear can arise in virtually anyone, and for a wide variety of reasons. We find things to fear in our actions, in our decisions, and in our new experiences. We find things to fear in our friends, our neighbors, and our bosses. We find things to fear in people we have never met or may never meet again. "Will I be respected? Will they impose upon me? Will they ignore me?"

Do you remember how scared you were the first time you jumped off a diving board? Went on your first date? Arrived for your first job interview? Flew on an airplane for the first time?

In most of those instances, you likely overcame your fear long enough to do what was necessary to experience the resulting benefit.

- You were willing to endure the fear of an interview to possibly obtain that new job and a higher income.
- You were willing to step aboard what you envisioned as that "long, silver, death tube" to fly across the country to your brother's wedding.
- I had to overcome the fear of playing the piano in front of people so I could enjoy creating music with other musicians. I had to learn to ignore my sweaty palms and trembling legs, forget the fact that people were watching me, and concentrate on the techniques required to play the music well.

Fear can give anyone a feeling of being trapped, helpless or in danger. It's easy to let your mind manufacture all kinds of reasons to be anxious or afraid, such as

fear of getting too close	fear of making a mistake
fear of what others think	fear of facing the truth
fear of rejection	fear of secrets being exposed
fear of conflict	fear of being misunderstood
fear of being disliked	fear of abandonment
fear of never getting it right	fear of vulnerability
fear of declining health	fear of never feeling safe again

When you have to do anything that takes you out of your comfort zone, fear tends to exaggerate and make things seem more difficult. You fear becoming overwhelmed when there is too much to do. Many of the things required of you are done under the stress of obligation or necessity, and you worry about your ability to do those things that life demands of you.

Just the thought of making a phone call to anyone intimidates me. I don't mind receiving phone calls, but the thought of calling someone, especially a stranger, to get a question answered or a business issue resolved sends me into a tizzy. What if I make a fool of myself? What if I fumble my words and don't ask the right questions? Will I be criticized for sounding stupid and wasting their time? Simply calling a friend unsettles me because I'm afraid my call will be an unwelcome intrusion. Even leaving a message on an answering machine makes me uneasy.

If you're always listening to that what-if voice in your head, you lose the ability to be in the moment and accomplish the task set before you. Thankfully, contacting friends has become easier for me with the magic of text messaging. As for calling strangers about business matters, I settle my nerves by writing down or practicing what I need to ask to obtain the information I need. Then I command myself, "Just do it!"

As a piano accompanist, fear of making a mistake sometimes unnerved me. I was playing in a Christmas concert with a fifty-piece orchestra and a 120-voice choir. Everything was going well until a sudden mishap caused me to panic. As I began to play the next song, I realized the orchestra was playing something different! I had placed the music in my notebook out of order. The song I should have been playing with the orchestra was quite difficult, and I was already nervous about messing it up. Missing those first lines was disastrous for me. By the time I found the right page, it was too late to make a graceful entrance into the awkward rhythm of the piece. I sat there, stunned.

As far as I know, only two people recognized that something was wrong: the music director, who glanced my way and saw the "deer in the headlights" look on my face, and the senior pastor, who was seated right next to the piano, heard my strangled gasp, and saw me frantically flipping pages. Fortunately, the absent piano part wasn't disastrous to the overall musical result. Only my tender ego was damaged as I sat there listening to the orchestra go on without me.

When you're afraid, your brain is busy kicking out a lot of adrenaline to deal with the stress in your body, making it impossible to make rational decisions. This was certainly the case in that startling concert moment when I became momentarily disoriented. I couldn't think clearly enough to quickly realize what was wrong and find my place in the music. It took the full duration of that instrumental composition for me to settle down and quietly prepare for the next concert piece.

Trapped in Fear

When you're afraid, you instinctively devise defenses to protect yourself and behave in ways that make you look better than you feel.

- If you fear that you're not engaging or popular, you might put a lot of energy into trying to please everyone.

- If you fear you're an annoyance, you might simply become passive and quiet.
- If you fear you're not smart enough or strong enough, you might push yourself to overachieve, becoming a workaholic or pushing your risk-taking behaviors to the brink of calamity.

In that uncomfortable concert moment, I put on my professional face and pretended I knew exactly what I was doing. Nobody could hear the rapid beating of my heart or see my trembling hands. Fortunately for my damaged ego, we performed the entire concert again the next night, and I was able to redeem myself gloriously!

When you hide behind your carefully crafted defenses, your fears seem more under control. You can become quite adept at pretending you aren't afraid as you perfect your many excuses for not taking a step toward what frightens you.

- You don't allow yourself to get too close to people because you're afraid your guilty secrets will be exposed.
- You don't express a legitimate need or desire because you fear becoming a problem or an inconvenience to someone.
- You dismiss the problem, saying you've never been good at something when in fact you're afraid your imperfections will become visible.
- You don't offer personal opinions for fear of being criticized or ridiculed.
- You justify any delay in resolving a problem by blaming your spouse, your friends, or your circumstances.
- You argue and defend yourself instead of accepting personal responsibility.

It's vital to remember that your fears and defenses have developed over time in reaction to real or imagined threats, and they are rooted in your irrational beliefs about yourself and others. Although your fears do not decrease your value as a person, they can destroy your self-confidence.

When Moses was leading the people of Israel out of Egypt, they came to a disheartening obstacle: the Red Sea. They believed their situation was totally hopeless with the sea blocking their way and the Egyptian army coming up fast behind them. When God ordered Moses and the people to move forward, they were certain they were all going to die right there at the edge of the sea.

The Israelites had been unenthusiastic throughout their journey out of Egypt. God knew that, but He didn't want them to look at the sea. He wanted them to look at Him and trust in what He could do. He knew they would experience His power in this situation by taking a step forward into that forbidding sea.

When your mind is clouded by fear and depression, all you can see is a problem too big to conquer and a pathway strewn with nothing but broken dreams and defeated plans. Although you may understand that God is trying to get you to face a problem area you need to change, such as a relationship, an attitude, or an addiction, it seems too scary and you don't want to go there. You would rather cling to the comfort and security of the familiar—familiar pain, familiar struggle, familiar patterns of thinking and doing. That's when you shut God out and run back to your familiar hiding places.

Fortunately, the Israelites were able to momentarily set aside their fear and timidly step into the cold, dark water. Then an amazing thing happened. The sea parted and the Israelites walked through on dry ground. By the time all of them arrived safely on the other side, the entire Egyptian army had entered the open sea bed and was drowned when God released those mountainous walls of water. I wonder what the Israelites were thinking then![40]

With God on your side, you're designed to win. He believes in you and has given you certain abilities, knowledge, skills, and talents to use in the plan He has for you.

Many of the Psalms were written by the trembling hand of David, who lived in the shadow of fear for years while on the run from King Saul. Notice David's response to fear in Psalm 56:3 (NCV): "When I am afraid, I will trust you."

Admit Your Fear

You must first admit that you're afraid. You have to let go of all of your security blankets that help you feel safe and comfortable, and all of those lies that you've been telling yourself. You need to be desperate enough to come to the end of yourself and open your mind to the challenging thought of trusting God to lead you out of the darkness of fear and into the light of His loving care.

The Israelites probably ran for their lives across the bottom of the Red Sea, still believing they couldn't possibly escape. In spite of this miracle, they didn't learn their lesson about trusting God for the results. We read later in the Old Testament (Numbers 13) the story of Joshua and Caleb, who led a group of scouts to explore the land of Canaan, which God had promised to the Israelites. Moses instructed them to see what the land looked like, find out if there were many inhabitants, discern whether the people were strong or weak, and locate any fruit in the land. After exploring the land for forty days, the men came back with bundles of fruit and stated the land was fertile, but ...

There's always a *but* when we're uncertain and afraid. Upon their return from exploring the land, the scouts' report was quite pessimistic even though they were aware this land had been promised to them by Jehovah. Despite the assurance from Joshua and Caleb that they were strong enough and capable enough to conquer the land with God's help, the scouts stalled and whined about the obstacles awaiting them. "The land is too large for us to occupy, and the cities are surrounded by walls. The people are strong, and our enemies occupy much of the land. Worse yet, there are giants living there! We looked like grasshoppers beside them. There's no way we can conquer this land and its people. We'd be better off staying in Egypt!"

Even though they believed God would rescue them from Egypt, they now believed they were being set up for failure because of what their fear had shown them. The devastating result of their rejection of God's promise and provision was that all of the Israelites were sentenced to forty years of wandering in the harsh wilderness until everyone over age twenty had died, thus barring the naysayers from entering the Promised Land. Even Moses had to stay behind because both he and his brother Aaron had broken faith with God by striking the rock at Meribah to obtain water. Moses had to spend the last breaths of his life climbing a distant mountain to view the Promised Land. Rather than stepping proudly onto the Promised Land, he could only take one last look from afar at what might have been.

Gain the Right Focus

One of the most frequently found commands in scripture is "Don't be afraid." The word *fear* and its related synonyms occur at least 260 times in scripture.

> You are my servant; I have chosen you and have not rejected you. So do not fear, for I am with you; do not be dismayed, for I am your God. (Isaiah 41:9-10)

The next time you're feeling afraid, pay attention to what you're focusing on. What are some things that fear is preventing you from achieving? Sometimes you need to take a step back and remind yourself of what you really want to accomplish. Then, when you do meet an obstacle, it's not going to slow you down. You'll be focusing on where you want to go and how you will get there. Instead of thinking of each fearful situation as a crisis to back away from, think of it as a challenging opportunity to try something new. Exercise your faith rather than your fear! God will not place anything into your life that is too hard for you to handle. It's only when you come to the end of yourself that you realize your only hope is to turn away from fear and toward God's gift of faith.

- Fear and faith cannot operate simultaneously.
- Fear feeds and thrives on feelings; faith is a deliberate choice and does not operate on feelings.
- Fear looks inward and finds instability; faith looks toward God and finds comfort and security.[41]

> Have I not commanded you? Be strong and courageous. Do not be afraid; do not be discouraged, for the Lord your God will be with you wherever you go. (Joshua 1:9)

God spoke these encouraging words to Joshua, who was about to lead the Israelites into the Promised Land after their forty years in the wilderness, and He's speaking these same words to you today.

Shame: The Five-Letter Word

Flooded with fear, anger, violence, hatred, and uncertainty, the world we live in has become unpredictable, undependable, and unforgiving. When we depend on the world to meet our needs, we're especially susceptible to fear and shame.

Fear and shame often go hand in hand. We're either afraid of being shamed, or we're ashamed of being afraid.

- Fear can discourage and debilitate us by exaggerating the unknown we can't see and filling our minds with horrifying images of red-eyed monsters that appear unworldly and uncontrollable.
- Shame can diminish and devastate us because we believe that red-eyed monster is us!

When that monster shoves you to the floor and screams in your ears that you're not good enough, you tell yourself you should stand up and fight back. Unfortunately, you're too afraid to do anything but curl up into the fetal position and hope the humiliation and terror will end soon.

- Fear tells you that something bad could happen; shame tells you that you are the cause of something bad.
- Fear says you'll make a mistake; shame says you are a mistake.
- Fear says others will think you're stupid; shame says you are stupid.
- The result of fear is paralysis; the result of shame is self-condemnation.

Shame is one of the most intense and debilitating feelings a person can experience because it combines other painful emotions such as anger, fear, bitterness, and hate. Anyone who has struggled with depression or anxiety has probably struggled with shame as well. As discussed in chapter 2, we create an image of who we should be early in life based on the beliefs and ideals of the people we loved and respected. When we believe we don't measure up to those ideal images, we feel inferior or deficient.[42]

Shame caused me to want to bury my head and disappear. I believed no one would want to get close to me, thus justifying my pushing them away. I deliberately avoided returning a phone call, backed out of a social event, called in sick for a job interview, or snubbed a former friend in a retail store, all because I was experiencing some sense of shame. I avoided social gatherings for fear of drawing unwanted attention to my perceived flaws. I tried to disguise my shame by becoming a perfectionist, believing I could hide my fear of failing, making mistakes, not meeting people's expectations, or being criticized.

Shame about being human has been passed down from generation to generation. In your early years of learning about life, you did nothing to be ashamed of. You were just a kid, a new little human who was being introduced to the complications of life by other already flawed individuals. You did the best you could to understand what was happening in your home and community. Only because of your immaturity and clumsiness about life was your heart broken and your tender mind thoughtlessly and randomly molded by those around you. You unknowingly incorporated a set of rules or social norms regarding your actions, thoughts, and feelings, which you judged to be right or wrong.

The emotional experience of shame is fueled by judgmental self-talk that was learned at a young age. Brené Brown states that the messages you tell yourself are always a variation of "I'm never good enough."

- I'm not good, pretty, talented, successful, rich, caring, skinny, masculine/feminine, or creative enough.
- I'm so stupid. I can't do anything right.
- I can change to fit in if I have to.
- No one can ever find out about *my private secret.*[43]

When you focus inward and tell yourself how wrong you are, you automatically believe you're always in the spotlight and everyone is looking at you. If you dress casually for an event only to discover upon arrival that everyone else is dressed up, you believe everyone is looking at you and whispering about your lack of sophistication.

Although you can't see your emotional pain like you can see a skinned knee, it's just as real and painful. The difference is that you can calm yourself over a skinned knee because you know what caused the pain: that sidewalk crack tripped you and sent you crashing into the unforgiving concrete! You also know that a fresh band aid and time will ease the pain.

You don't have the same confidence about your emotional pain because it doesn't seem to have a beginning or an end, especially if it's a pain that has followed you since childhood. When there's an elusive sense of sadness, fear, or shame lurking in the hidden corners of your heart, or you keep hearing those whiny voices in your mind saying you're not good enough, it's too exhausting to even try to understand it.

Brené Brown advises that, if you are out there looking for reasons why you're unworthy or not good enough, you're always going to find them!

Recognize and Refute Your Shame

It's important to give a name to what you're feeling, whether it's guilt, sadness, loneliness, shame, worthlessness, or fear. Even if you can only come up with one word—depressed—that's a place to start rather than stuffing your feelings and trying to ignore them.

Although shame can be experienced in different physical and emotional ways, there are some general indicators that can help in identifying your shame and bringing it into the light.

Urge to Emotionally Isolate

Researchers including Linda M. Hartling, the director of the Human Dignity and Humiliation Studies (HumanDHS), and Brené Brown indicate there are three common signs that you're isolating yourself:

- **moving away** from others by withdrawing, being silent, and keeping secrets;
- **moving toward** unhealthy relationships by trying to appease and people please; and
- **moving against** others by being aggressive and trying to restore one's dignity by overpowering others—fighting shame with shame.

Being aware of your typical knee-jerk reactions increases your chance of pausing, reflecting, and learning to recognize your specific shame triggers so you can respond in a more courageous and intentional way.[44]

Physical Manifestations

In addition to the emotional isolation of shame, there are almost always physical indicators such as

- flushed cheeks,
- dizziness,
- sweaty palms,
- chest constriction, or
- an inability to make eye contact.

These symptoms are similar to the sensation of panic, which triggers a fight-or-flight response in the body. Physically, you interpret both panic and shame as the threat of danger.[45]

Being able to label the specific feeling and its physical indicators helps you move away from the emotion and toward a solution. Once you've named your feeling, you've begun to think!

- What's going through your mind?
- Are you hearing messages about who you are instead of what you've done?
- Are you thinking "I'm a failure" instead of "I failed at that project"?

When you begin to refute those unhealthy beliefs about yourself, you can start to experience what's happening right now instead of feeling inferior because of some faulty, repetitive message from your past.

Start telling yourself the truth. Are you actually that incompetent, inadequate so-and-so you believe you are? No! You're smart, you're dependable, you have a special skill, and you are persistent. If you look at your self-talk with the objective eyes of a scientist—or better yet, through the loving eyes of your Creator—you'll be able to punch holes in those self-defeating beliefs and start believing in the person God created you to become.

> Everything is either an opportunity to grow or an obstacle to keep you from growing. You get to choose.
> —Wayne W. Dyer[46]

Vulnerability: The Unspoken Word

Vulnerability comes from the Latin word for *wound, vulnus.* Vulnerability is commonly interpreted as being open or susceptible to injury or exposure. I don't even like to think about the word, much less speak it or write it. I tend to think that showing vulnerability makes me seem weak, inadequate, and flawed—yet I view other people's willingness to be vulnerable as strength and courage. It's their vulnerability that actually draws me to them.

In order for connection to happen, vulnerability is a necessity. In her book *Daring Greatly,* Brené Brown asserts that "Vulnerability is about showing up and being seen. It's tough to do that when you're terrified about what people might see or think." [47]

> Why am I afraid to tell you who I am? If I tell you who I am, you may not like who I am, and it is all that I have.
> —John Powell, S.J.[48]

When you're hiding behind the walls you erect and the armor you put on to protect yourself from exposure to others, you shut off connection with people. Instead of exposing what you believe is your inadequacy and uncertainty, you tend to become defensive or controlling, pretending that you're strong and capable. Pretending who you are can only thicken the walls you've built and prevent you from entering intimate relationships.

Vulnerability is not a weakness, and neither is it a sympathy-seeking tool. To be vulnerable doesn't mean you blurt out every personal failing or fear to anyone around you. Emoting just for the sake of sharing without boundaries or being clear about your intentions and expectations isn't useful or effective. You must be aware of who you're talking to and whether or not you're sharing your vulnerable moment with one of your safe people.

Think about those relationships that mean the most to you. Were you able to connect deeply with someone by being defensive or argumentative? Probably not. The relationships that provide true connection and meaning to your life are those where you've been willing to expose your fear, your uncertainty, your deepest hurts, and your greatest joys. Ms. Brown further states that it is through vulnerability that "we learn how to adapt to change, enter difficult conversations, accept constructive feedback, and bounce back from those unwelcome blows to our egos that occasionally surprise and bewilder us."

Being vulnerable never comes with guarantees. Instead, it's having the courage to show up when you can't control the outcome. Courage doesn't eliminate fear, but vulnerability coupled with courage may allow you to perform musically before a live audience, publish your first book, launch a new business, tell someone you love him or her, put a boundary in place, hold the hand of someone in despair, or reach out to let others know that you're terrified about a recent health diagnosis. Although fear or shame may try to paralyze you, courage and vulnerability allow you to put one foot in front of the other.[49]

No one can make you feel inferior without your consent.
—Eleanor Roosevelt[50]

Who Are Your Safe People?

Vulnerability requires not only courage but also trust. Brené Brown states that we need to trust to be vulnerable, and we need to be vulnerable to build trust. Both of these learning processes develop over time and involve risk. This is why it's vitally important to pursue the process of understanding who you are, what you think, and how you feel, as well as learn to recognize the safe people in your life.

Does the person with whom you are bearing your soul or setting a new boundary respect your vulnerability or honor the boundary lines you've drawn? If so, this is the kind of person you want in your life. If not, you may want to reevaluate the importance of this relationship, or perhaps even end it.

How do you go about finding these safe people? First look in the obvious places: your family, your coworkers, your church, your buddies on the bowling team, or the people in your study group or book club. There's no sure way to know that a particular person will turn out to be trustworthy. However, there are certain behavioral traits to watch for, both healthy and unhealthy, which can lead you to the right people. Knowing the difference means that you can enter into relationships with people who are good for you and avoid those who aren't.

Who Are the Untrustworthy People?

When you're depressed and desperate, you can easily disregard all of the outward and inward signs that indicate whether or not a person can be trusted. It's tempting to trust the wrong people with your deepest thoughts when they make you feel appreciated and understood. It's important to carefully evaluate the person before handing over your total trust in them. How do you spot someone who is untrustworthy?

- **Untrustworthy people demand trust instead of earning it.** These people often insist that you should trust them right away, and they act hurt or defensive if you don't. Trust can only be built over time. It grows when you experience consistent, caring behavior.
- **Untrustworthy people with an agenda know what to say to get you hooked.** They tell you what you want to hear, making it attractive to follow their lead. They sense or look for those areas where you are lacking in confidence and self-esteem, and they easily pick up on those things you long to believe about yourself.
- **Untrustworthy people do not like to admit their weaknesses.** Being open and vulnerable is essential to a relationship. Sometimes people will try to hide their weaknesses by focusing on your weaknesses instead. Putting you down is an easy way to build themselves up. If you are the one with the problems, then they can feel superior.[51]

How Do You Recognize the Safe People?

A safe person is someone you can depend on, someone who is honest and has your best interests at heart.

- They are likeable, humble, and easy to talk to. They say what needs to be said, and they mean what they say.
- They are respectful with their time and yours.
- They don't need to prove anything. They're willing to ask for help.
- They own their mistakes, apologize, and make amends.
- They don't feel the need to control those around them. They acknowledge that no means no.
- They don't whisper snide comments or participate in gossip. When told a secret, they keep it, and they expect the same of you.
- They're willing to provide helpful feedback and constructive criticism.
- They accept you just as you are, and they are who they say they are.
- They allow you to be on the outside who you are on the inside.
- Their life touches yours and leaves you better for it.

Brené Brown has presented a TED talk on "The Anatomy of Trust,"[52] which I highly recommend watching. She talks about jars of marbles, describing how it is the small things people say and do that communicate to you that you are important. These are the people whose faces light up when you walk into the room, and who have few if any agendas to change you. My friend Connie calls these your "nutritious" people.

Doctors Henry Cloud and John Townsend have written extensively about the importance of finding those people who are sympathetic and safe, there for you, on your side, pulling for you, and available and willing to comfort and advise you.[53]

Sympathy vs. Empathy

It's wonderful to have sympathetic or empathetic friends who know you well: what's important to you, your perspective on life, and those life struggles that drag you down and discourage you. Even though sympathy and empathy are quite similar, they are often confused with each other. What's the difference?

Both sympathetic and empathetic people might acknowledge your particular struggle and provide comfort, assurance, and possibly advice, but there is a subtle difference between the two.

Although a sympathetic friend feels sorry for your hardship and genuinely hopes things will improve for you, she isn't always able to understand your struggle or sense your deep emotions. As a result, she often feels inadequate to respond to your dilemma and can only offer words of comfort in an attempt to defuse your pain.

I experienced an example of this one winter. Someone at church had asked why I hadn't been there for the previous few weeks. I was only willing to answer that I was struggling again with depression and was unable to drag myself off the couch. Her advice was to buy a sun lamp, indicating that often helps people. It was evident that she truly wanted to help, but she had no clear understanding of the suffocating effect of depression. In her sincere effort to defuse my pain, she stated, "At least you don't have several grandkids moping around the house with you." As if that happy thought could relieve my depression! If you hear the words "at least" in response to whatever dilemma or difficulty you're describing, you may be hearing sympathy, but it's not empathy.

Empathy comes quietly in those unexpected moments when someone you've known for only a short time remembers your name and a bit of your story, or when your friend exhibits extreme patience with your lack of know-how in a particular situation and gently provides the information you need without ridicule or humiliation.

An empathetic person is able to put herself in your shoes, viewing and feeling your situation from your perspective without having your exact feelings, thoughts, and experiences fully and explicitly communicated.

In her TED Talk on "The Power of Vulnerability," Brené Brown described empathy this way: "Empathy is a choice, and it's a vulnerable choice. In order to connect with you, I have to connect with something in myself that knows that feeling."[54]

I've gratefully experienced this kind of connection more than once. A uniquely meaningful moment for me occurred recently on a Caribbean cruise sponsored by Kathy Troccoli, the Christian singer I've mentioned earlier. I had the opportunity to speak with her privately for several minutes. As I told her a bit about Jesus' request that I walk away from the musical life I'd been enjoying and follow Him, her response was precious. Her eyes and mind were focused directly on me. She asked only one simple question to obtain a clarifying detail. She spoke no other words as I continued my story, but I saw the tears she was wiping from her eyes. It was clear that she deeply understood and felt my agony in choosing to love my Lord more than my music, to walk away from my safe place behind the piano, and to bravely face the uncertainty ahead. Kathy needed no words to connect with me. Her sensitive tears and lingering, comforting hug were enough. That's empathy.

Choose Self-forgiveness over Self-condemnation

You can accept who you are now instead of feeling shame about who you thought you were. You can learn to be more open with people instead of worrying about what they might think of you. When you begin to see that you are simply human like everybody else, you will be able to engage in more comfortable connections with other people. That's the beginning of vulnerability … and healing.

Second Corinthians 10:5 states that true freedom from fear and shame demands that every thought, feeling, and belief must be opened to examination. Shame can only survive if you don't acknowledge it or talk about it. For shame to exist, you need secrecy, isolation, and a fear of judgment by others. If you can share your story with someone who responds with empathy, comfort, and understanding, then shame cannot survive.

Jesus is quite intentional in the ways and times He allows us to experience moments of agony and uncertainty. He often allows the desperation of fear and shame to settle in or, as in the case of a memory, return so He can bring it into the light. While I was writing this chapter, Jesus brought me a gift: another of those long-forgotten memories filled with pain. (Thanks, Jesus.) Although that incident isn't a big deal now, I did shed some tears as I relived and wrote about the deep hurt I'd felt in that past moment.

When I was in my mid-twenties and in Iowa for a weekend visit, one of the men in my home church approached me and asked rather bluntly, "Why aren't you married yet?" That was back in the days when it was commonly expected that all females would complete their schooling and then settle down with a husband and a houseful of kids. I had already participated in the weddings of friends and experienced the pain that naturally comes when those friends become busy with their exciting new lives. I desperately wanted to be married so I could experience that new life for myself and cancel out the old, familiar sense of abandonment.

If someone were to ask me today why I'm not married, I'd probably laugh. At the time, though, that thoughtless remark tugged rudely at the aching emptiness in my heart. I don't recall if I offered any reply to that man, but I'm sure the thought darkening my mind was, "Because nobody wants me." That hurt.

Though initially painful, honest unmasking before the Lord is the only way to see wounds healed, distorted thoughts untwisted, and false beliefs eliminated.[55] I admit that when I replayed that long-ago memory in my mind, I cried a little as I relived my distress in that moment. I also chuckled a bit as I forgave that dear man and released myself from any lingering insult or pain.

Regardless of where you are in your battle with shame or fear, be gentle with yourself. No shame story has to define you, and you don't have to continue in that role. Although you may look back at portions of your past with some regret and remorse, it's important to realize that you were doing the best you could at the time given the resources, knowledge, and life skills available to you.

Instead of allowing yourself to continue living with fear or shame, ask yourself some rational questions.

- What does the emotion you're feeling mean?
- Focus on what you're thinking. Are you upset about something you don't like about yourself?
- Why don't you like that thing about yourself? Is it because of an ideal or expectation you've placed on yourself?
- Is that ideal important to anyone besides you? Why is it important? Where did it come from?
- What actions would you take if that ideal was no longer important? What would happen if you decided to eliminate that ideal as an old garment and try on a new outfit?
- What would change if you discarded that ideal? How would you show up differently? Would you be able to move around with a sense of confidence about yourself?

As you grow and mature in your understanding of life, you will learn that those critical thoughts that have kept you isolated and defeated have only as much power over you as you will allow.

Adversity is an effective tool that God can use in helping you develop a strong faith. He walks with each one of us through fearful situations and moments of discomfort and shame. As you learn to obey His Word and allow it to saturate your thoughts, you will find that each trial becomes another step forward on that foggy bridge, bringing you ever closer to a stronger, deeper faith.[56]

Kathy Troccoli has written these words.

> Becoming the person God longs for us to be doesn't happen easily or quickly. No one waves a magic wand over your head and—voila—the Proverbs 31 woman emerges. It's a process of walking each day with Him. Asking Him to penetrate your soul. Giving Him permission to mold you, change you, shake you, move you.[57]

Faith is described in Hebrews 11:1 as being "certain of what we do not see." It's not just taking a leap into the darkness hoping for good results. It's true that fear and shame can grab and shake our emotions, but faith can take hold of our fear and shame, pry them loose, and place them gently into the healing hands of our Creator and Lord.

Face in the Mirror

As I sat alone one day
just weeping bitter tears,
someone took me by the hand
and whispered in my ear.
He talked with me and told me
my despair was in His hands.
He dried my tears and said
He loves me just the way I am.

He took me to a mirror, asking,
"Who is that you see?"
He showed me things about myself
that I had never seen.
"Who else is there in that reflection
looking back at you?"
That's when I saw His dazzling face,
and suddenly I knew:

Jesus! Master! There You are!
I thought You'd gone away.
I've been so sad and fearful
as I've looked for You each day.
He held me close and softly said,
"I'll never leave your side."
That's when I knew I'd found myself
by looking in His eyes.

Chapter 9
Are You Ready for Change?

Have you ever made a New Year's resolution and vowed that you would follow through no matter what? Did you follow through? Maybe for a couple of months? The problem with New Year's resolutions is that you don't really prepare yourself for change. Your resolutions tend to be based on a certain date on the calendar, but you don't plan ahead regarding how to stay on track for the coming months. Eventually your resolution slips back onto your forgotten wish list.

When you've tried and failed, it's easier to whine, "Nothing ever changes." Think again! If you live anywhere on this earth, the weather changes quite often. If you're breathing, the days of the week are constantly changing. If you eat a normal diet, the variety of foods you eat changes. If you're part of a family group, your sons, daughters, brothers, sisters, and parents change. TV shows change. Society's politics and morals change. Friends come and go like the seasons.

Is anyone ever ready for change? Probably not. Change isn't easy. I got stuck in just wishing things would get better. I was afraid I wouldn't be able to change. I got so bogged down by depression and the stresses of life that I could only groan, "I can't do that. It's too hard." I became discouraged by my brave experiments that didn't work, like my failed attempt to become someone different by moving from the chilly Midwest to the sweltering Deep South.

Change is difficult and uncertain, and there is no guarantee of success. You first want some proof that the change is even necessary. You believe that sameness equals safety and change equals danger. You know that what you're already doing isn't helpful, but at least it doesn't scare you!

If fear is the four-letter word and shame is the five-letter word, change is the six-letter word! You resist new behaviors, new ways of thinking, changes to your plans, changes in your circumstances, and changes in your lifestyle because of fear or shame. Change can threaten your relationships, your position, your sense of self-control, or your feelings of security.

You don't know how to live outside your protective shell of depression and shame because that's all you've ever known. You've become comfortable in the closely controlled atmosphere of your dusty, light-deprived secret rooms, and you have grown accustomed to the smell of your stinking thinking. Because fear and shame can paralyze and defeat you and have unwanted consequences, you resist change and remain tied to your old self.

It's not just the change that scares you but the imagined reality of what the change might bring. It's easy to believe that making any change is a huge task that can't be reversed if something goes wrong. You can't see it, touch it, feel it, or experience it. You can only assume what the outcome will be, but our assumptions are only 50 percent accurate at best! In reality, it's the thick fog in the air that blinds and frightens you, not the outcome you can't yet see at the other end of that foggy bridge.

What is it that you believe will never change? Let me guess. You believe you're unworthy and unlovable and all the other *un-* words you can think of to describe yourself. That's a lie from the mouth of Satan. He's a deceiver and a liar. Don't listen to him! He wants you to believe there's no hope for you. He's acutely aware that he can keep you down for as long as he can prevent you from seeing or hearing the truth. He's the master of darkness, and he knows how to break your focus and cause more confusion, anxiety, and distress.

Satan also knows the Truth! He knows that Jesus came to bring a whole new way of thinking and believing and behaving! Colossians 3:9–10 (NCV) reminds us as followers of Jesus Christ that "You have left your old sinful life and the things you did before. You have begun to live the new life, in which you are being made new and are becoming like the One who made you."

Our Lord and Savior never promised that change would be easy or quick. You have to go through the refiner's fire to burn away your faulty beliefs and stinking thinking, to cleanse the impurities from your attitudes, and to correct the flaws in your priorities and behaviors. I love the way this principle is expressed in The Message:

> My assumption is that you have paid careful attention to him [Christ], been well instructed in the truth precisely as we have it in Jesus. Since, then, we do not have the excuse of ignorance, everything—and I do mean everything— connected with that old way of life has to go. It's rotten through and through. Get rid of it! And then take on an entirely new way of life—a God-fashioned life, a life renewed from the inside and working itself into your conduct as God accurately reproduces his character in you. (Ephesians 4:20–24 MSG, emphasis added)

Changing Means Grieving

No change is easy, painless, or short-lived. Sigmund Freud[58] likened the process of change to the process of mourning the death of a loved one. In the work of changing yourself, you must leave behind a part of your old self to which you are strongly attached, even though it's all you have ever known. It won't be easy or painless.

You will need to go through stages of acceptance just like you do any other grieving process: two steps forward, one step back. Your choice is whether or not to pay the price for the improvement and work your way through the process. Each step forward is an act of faith in the idea that change is actually a good thing.

Stage 1: Don't Need To

When you're depressed, you are in a state of numbness and wonder how you can go on, if you can go on, and why you should go on. The world seems meaningless, and you don't even recognize your need to change. You're simply clinging to the old thoughts, behaviors, and memories as you try to find a way to get through each day.

Stage 2: Shouldn't Have To

You're angry that you even have to change. You may even shout, "Where is God in this?" Good or bad, anger is a necessary stage of the change process. It can muster up a kind of strength that can move you to action.

Stage 3: Don't Want To

Just as you're about to take a step forward, you become afraid you might fail. You know it will hurt to have your fingers pried from those things that have become too comfortable or important. This could be the fear of the alcoholic who still believes she needs the drink, or the abused woman who believes she needs the man who's abusing her, or the depressed woman who believes she needs her depression to obtain attention and assurance.

Stage 4: Exchange Your Why for What

When Jesus allows your life to include disappointment, pain, and discouragement, use the opportunity to ask Him better questions! Ask what He wants you to learn through this difficulty. Instead of asking "Why me?" or "Why now?" ask God what He's trying to teach you. When you ask why, you're thinking like a victim. When you ask what or how, you're proactively searching for a solution—God's solution. Asking Him to show you what He wants to teach you is accepting responsibility for taking the next step toward the freedom He offers.

God's Steady and Sure Pathway

I began my adult life dreaming of great things to come, but those dreams were born in childhood when everything seemed possible. Sunday school teachers assured me that God had a wonderful plan for my life. In my world of small-town Iowa, I was eagerly practicing my piano lessons with the dream of having a successful concert ministry or becoming a beloved piano teacher like my mom. What my encouragers did not tell me was that my plans and God's plans would probably not follow the same path! Life rarely goes the way we planned.

Although I found joy and a sense of accomplishment in playing all styles of music with many talented musicians, I remained in a dark hole emotionally. Some of the circumstances of my life had obviously changed, but I continued to whine that nothing ever changed.

Remarkably, I didn't begin to understand until much later in my life that God had been consistently and lovingly opening doors to my musical talent not so much to improve my musicianship or open a path to that music career I had dreamed of, but specifically to teach me and guide me in His ways and build my self-confidence through those agonizing years of deep depression. It wasn't really about the music at all! That was simply the structure He used to begin putting the chaotic notes of my life together and working to restore me to emotional and spiritual health.

You may be looking for steps that tell you what to do first, next, and last before you commit to any kind of movement out of your deep rut. Reading psychological information or books like this one can certainly provide useful ideas and tools to get you started. But wanting to know everything before trying to change can cause you to put off actually making changes while you continue looking for and hoping for some easy solution.

It's easy to convince yourself that making one small change won't make any difference in the long run, so you give up before you even start, believing it would be a waste of time and effort. You want to see change before actually choosing to make change!

As psychologist Michael D. Yapko states in his book *Breaking the Patterns of Depression*, "If you keep doing things in the same crummy way, you'll keep getting the same crummy results."[59]

If you change your identity or habits too quickly and become someone radically different overnight, you will feel as if you've lost your sense of self. It's better, and less stressful, to expand your identity gradually, one small step at a time. James Clear, in his book *Atomic Habits*, states that you can make tiny changes and see remarkable results![60]

Once your problem drives you to God, He will reveal what He wants you to learn. He can focus your attention on those pieces of life that you didn't know were even important in the growing, maturing process:

- the choices you make,
- the relationships you cultivate,

- the boundaries you set,
- the beliefs that keep you stuck, and
- the thoughts you think.

Jesus' Spirit will teach you day by day, moment by moment, what you need to know and how to become who He designed you to be. If you're resistant to God's direction to put away the credit card, to walk past the donut shop, to throttle your urge to join in with the gossipers, or to turn off the TV and focus on your children, God may wait longer to do His good pleasure in you. His greatest desire is that you grow in your knowledge of Him as you mature in your ability to do life as a child of the King.

Action Comes Before Motivation

Change is an action word. Change is the key to getting out of your deep rut even when you don't feel like making the effort. Change is possible and necessary, but change will almost never happen if you don't take the first step forward.

One of the most common problems with depression is that your mood can rob you of the will to do anything. You feel blah all the time and don't even want to get out of bed. You're busy accusing yourself of being lazy or worthless. It's easier to go back to sleep than to make a different choice. Because of the lower levels of serotonin in your system, your brain is sluggish and unable to send the appropriate messages to your motor nerves. Just getting your toes to wiggle seems like too much work.

If you're waiting until you feel "in the mood" to do something, you'll automatically put it off because you never feel like it! If you're waiting for someone else to come along and push you forward, you may have to wait a long time. Dr. David Burns wrote, "If you want to get motivated, then start taking action. Motivation does not come first, action does!"[61]

You can think all day about starting a walking regimen to lose weight, but it will never happen until you take that first step out the door or onto the treadmill. This was proven to me each time I had to mow the lawn at the home I owned for thirty-two years. It was a large lawn, and I had no riding lawn mower or handyman to do the job. I had to walk numerous laps around the double lot. Some days, especially after a stressful day at work, I struggled to force myself out the door and get started. I eventually discovered that once I took that first step away from the couch and put on my lawn-mowing shoes, I could make it all the way to the garage, fill the mower with gas, put in my earplugs, and pull the cord. By then, there was no turning back. Each week I was surprised that the ninety-minute walk in the fresh air improved my mood significantly. When I finally returned the mower to the garage and admired my freshly mowed lawn, I was exhausted but fully satisfied. Finishing was such a huge accomplishment that I usually rewarded myself with a cool shower, a cold mug of water, and some ice cream. Great motivation!

Your perspective on life is linked to what you do, where and when you do it, how you do it, and how it makes you feel. It's easier to change what you're doing than to change how you're feeling or what you're thinking. Doing something as simple as going through that pile of unopened mail or washing that sink full of dirty dishes can provide the action you need to keep moving and accomplish additional tasks.

Here is a short list of ideas to get yourself moving.

- **Get up and turn on the lights.** You might not feel like it, but bright light has been shown to have an antidepressant effect. Try to get outside in the sunlight for at least a half hour each day.
- **Move!** Be active right away. Mild exercise gets the blood flowing and transports more oxygen throughout your body (especially to your brain), helping you feel more mentally alert.
- **Listen to some energetic music.** Often just an upbeat rhythm and Christian-based lyrics can elevate your mood and make you feel more like moving your feet.
- **Change your routine.** Choose a different route to work or church, or eat at a different restaurant. Do anything that brings variation to the "same old, same old" routine.
- **Seek out humor.** Watch a funny movie or get together with friends who make you laugh. Proverbs 17:22 tells us that "a cheerful heart is good medicine, but a crushed spirit dries up the bones."
- **Pursue interests and activities you enjoy.** My passion for music and playing the piano has brought me much joy and provided

a therapeutic release for my depression. Even though I'm not playing publicly, I do enjoy attending concerts and other musical events to lift my spirits.

Whenever I find myself unwilling to move beyond my inactivity and dark mood to accomplish something unpleasant that must be done, I take myself by the hand and firmly state, "Just get up and do it!" Although that doesn't always work, it usually turns my mind away from feeling sorry for myself. Once I've managed to move my fingers and toes and elevate my mood a bit, I've generated enough energy to begin the real work of change.

The prophet Isaiah wrote, "He gives strength to the weary and increases the power of the weak" (Isaiah 40:29). God's energy and strength brings tangible, noticeable change and is available continuously, every moment of every day.

The Tried-and-True "To Do" List

Are you a list maker? Do you make lists to remind you of places you need to go, items you need to purchase, phone calls you need to make, or tasks you must complete within a specific time frame? Have you ever made a list of areas in your emotional or spiritual life that you need or want to change? Below are a few areas of change from chapter 6 on choices that might resonate with you.

- I want to stop a bad habit—smoking, drinking, overeating.
- I want to stop procrastinating.
- I want to get out of debt.
- I want to manage my anger.
- I want to find a way out of this abusive relationship.
- I want to ...

Take some time to think about how you can fill in the blank or add to the list. Focus your list on particular areas that are affecting your thinking, your attitudes, your relationships, or your walk with the Lord. Once you begin spending time in His Word, you will see changes as His Word begins to transform your thinking.

One advantage I've found in my seasons of depression is that the particular problems, concerns, wrong attitudes, or irresponsible thinking that I refuse to think about when I'm feeling good are the very things that come into sharp focus when I'm depressed. It's those things I tend to ruminate on and worry over while in a dark mood. Once I recognized this pattern, I trained myself during those times of wallowing in depression to take special note of those dark thoughts, problems, and obstacles and write them down. Once the depression subsided and I could think more rationally, I would look back at what I'd written and focus on new ways of changing those upsetting situations or eliminating those troublesome behaviors. In the process:

- I named the insecurities that were preventing change.
- I worked to understand the old beliefs that contributed to my self-defeating thoughts.
- I practiced transparency and truthfulness about my dark thoughts.
- I worked on building important relationships with the safe people I would need when I once again became stranded in the fog of depression.

Change begins when you crack open the door to your secret room and begin to face your brokenness. It might seem too painful today, too demanding, or too hopeless. Although you might occasionally slip back into thinking that you're doomed to a life of failure, you must keep trying to climb out of that pit, one inch at a time!

Take a lesson from this inventor who never stopped trying.

> I have not failed 10,000 times. I've just found 10,000 ways that won't work.[62]
>
> —Thomas Edison

Looking for Safe Harbor

Restless, seeking, always moving,
like a wave upon the sea,
pressing cautiously ahead,
ever longing to break free.

Weary of the wind and chaos,
dreaming of the sun-drenched sand,
rushing past the foaming crest
with not a thought of harm, nor plan.

Smashing hard against the rocks,
this wave can go no farther.
It must retreat and try again,
still looking for safe harbor.

Are We There Yet?

Do you remember those trips to Grandma's house when you were young and impatient? You may have sounded like a broken record, asking over and over, "Are we there yet?" Did it make the trip go faster? Nope!

The chief complaint of those trying to change their ways is, "Why does it have to take so long?" The answer is: it just does. There are no shortcuts. The Israelites were forced to wander in the wilderness for forty years because they hadn't been willing to heed God's warnings and directions for their lives. Of course, they whined the whole time: "When will this be over? How much farther must we go? Are we there yet?"

There were certainly no shortcuts for Jonah, who decided he'd make a two-thousand-mile journey by ship to Tarsus to avoid God's command to walk to Nineveh and preach salvation to his nation's worst enemy. God knew where to find him, and He detained Jonah for three days and nights in the belly of a big fish to force him to think about what he was doing.

Once Jonah agreed that he had messed up and the fish had deposited him onto the shore in Joppa, where he had begun his attempt to escape, he still had to walk those five hundred miles to Nineveh!

Wilderness experiences are carefully timed by God and are never accidents. Although the process of wandering through the wilderness of pain and confusion often seems useless, taking little steps in any direction can serve important purposes in God's plans:

- Wilderness cleans you out, scrubbing away old anger, self-condemnation, and bitterness so that deep cleansing can take place.
- Wilderness becomes a classroom where the Lord infuses you with a new perspective and molds you into a new identity.[63]

Wandering in the wilderness is never fun, but it can be a place to ditch the baggage from your past: your irrational beliefs about yourself, your old hiding behavior, or your self-imposed neediness.

Why did Jesus wait so long to provide answers for my deep pain and woe? He waited forty years to finally reveal to me the initial event that sent me into a lifelong tailspin through depression.

- Forty years of wandering in the wilderness of confusion and uncertainty
- Forty years of thinking that every damaged or lost relationship in my life was somehow my fault
- Forty years of believing that no one really loved or cared about me
- Forty years of chronic, often desperately hopeless depression
- Forty years ... wasted?

Think again! No life is wasted if the Lord Jesus is in it!

God understands our need to hide, and He provides a safe and effective hiding place for each of us in our wilderness wanderings. In Psalm 32:7 King David wrote, "You are my hiding place; you will protect me from trouble and surround me with songs of deliverance." In Psalm 9:9 he wrote, "The Lord is a refuge for the oppressed, a stronghold in times of trouble." He wasn't talking about those secret rooms where we like to stash our stuff!

When you know your life is hidden with Christ, you can run into His place of refuge at any time and find yourself protected from your fears, your pain, your shame, your vulnerability—whatever it is you need to hide from. God has promised to always be with you, to provide what you need when you need it, and to see you through the most uncertain and fearful hours of your life as you move forward on the path He has set for you.

Sometimes when I've found myself wandering again into the deep fog of depression, Jesus has reached down and pulled me free. At other times, He has met me there in the dark and kept me safe as I struggled to hear His voice and find my way back to Him. During those times when I didn't want to listen to His words of advice and correction, His still, small voice tenderly reminded me that He loves me. Even when I didn't sense His nearness, He covered me with His grace and sheltered me in His presence (Psalm 31:20).

Jesus always finds a way to break through my stubborn attitudes and show me what He longs for most: intimate relationship with me.

- He teaches me about His comfort for me as a needy child who just wants to be loved and snuggled.
- He provides opportunities and situations to learn the necessary lessons about living in this tough world.
- He provides for me financially in unexpected ways through various people He has called upon to care for me.
- He opens doors for me that bring me into contact with the people He knows I need for particular seasons of my emotional and spiritual growth.
- He allows me to go my own way at times, but He is always within reach when I realize that my way is headed for trouble.
- He laughs with me and cries with me.
- When my thoughts are dark, He is the light.
- When I feel alone, He comes close and whispers, "I'm right here; look at Me."
- He is never impatient when I stumble and turn away from Him. His hand is always outstretched and ready to draw me back into His sheltering embrace.

First Peter 5:10 assures us that we will be restored.

And the God of all grace, who called you to his eternal glory in Christ, after you have suffered a little while, will himself restore you and make you strong, firm and steadfast.

Change Doesn't Happen Quickly

Jesus is infinitely patient! He often has to wait until you've come to the end of yourself and your finite resources before you begin to hear His gentle whispers to come to Him and learn from Him. Once you choose to move in the direction God is leading and believe His promises, He will pursue His transforming work in you, no matter how long it takes.

What are the obstacles that have stopped you in your tracks and pushed you back into uncertainty and fear? Look again at that list you made of things in your life you want to change. Where are you feeling overwhelmed or stuck? What about your life is robbing you of peace?

- Is it a transition from being a happily married Mom to a divorced, single Mom with no job or means of support? Maybe you need to meet with a support group who understands your situation and can refer you to helpful resources.
- Is it a teenage son who has become involved in drugs and seems no longer manageable? Maybe you need to talk with a counselor.
- Is it a feeling of insecurity as you near retirement? Maybe you need to seek out a financial advisor.
- Is it a sudden weariness over the demands of single-handedly owning and keeping up a home? Maybe you need to explore the possibility of selling your house and moving into an apartment or townhouse.
- Are you being pulled in too many directions by the needs and demands of your family, your work, or your friends? Maybe you need to set some priorities or make different choices.
- Are you being dragged down by the people around you who are critical and manipulative? Maybe you need to set some boundaries and build a more encouraging support network.
- Is your irrational thinking keeping you immobilized and unable to see better alternatives? Maybe you need to monitor your

self-talk and begin noting and eliminating those situations that tend to paralyze your mind and drag you down.

You cannot change your destination overnight, but you can change your direction overnight.

—Jim Rohn[64]

I don't understand why Jesus has allowed depression to be a constant companion throughout my life. However, with the advantage of looking back on sixty-plus years of doing life, I can appreciate why it's taken so long to move forward. Actor Woody Harrelson has stated that "a grownup is a child with layers on."[65] I've had to strip away layer upon layer of buried hurt, anger, poor choices, learned habits, manipulative behaviors, and memories of bungled or misunderstood relationships. This has taken much time and struggle ... and many mistakes. That's part of the process of doing life!

Whenever I was asked to play a difficult piece of music, I couldn't skip over the hard parts and play only the easy stuff. I had to learn how to practice and to painstakingly work out in detail every wrong note, every complicated rhythm, and every clumsy fingering. I often had to play the same unwieldy passage over and over to master it. I then had to practice connecting it with the rest of the piece without stumbling. None of that work was fun. I still don't like practicing ... but I love the results!

Life is like that: hard, sometimes tedious practice with lots of blunders. God is working to transform you into that person He created you to be. He expects you to make mistakes, and He will use your mistakes to show you what you need to work on more diligently.

Are you willing to take lessons from the Master Teacher and learn the necessary rhythms of life that will ease your way through a difficult season? I suspect you would rather skip the hard parts and pretend your way through. That's the easy way to do life. But you would find that when you're faced with the next stressful situation that requires you to play the hard part while battling stage fright, you'll likely wish you had done the diligent practice.

Change is necessary for recovery. Jesus calls you to change! You can't choose to remain the same and still resolve your problems. At least twenty-eight times throughout Jesus' ministry, He stated, "I have come to change your hearts and lives." Jesus always keeps His promises!

Stop whining about how hard life is or how long it takes to change your behavior, your circumstances, or your thoughts. Latch onto God's power within you and His guidance for you. Ask Him what He wants you to focus on and change. Then start turning those small changes into small habits that will gradually refine and redefine you.

> When you change your thinking, you change your beliefs.
> When you change your beliefs, you change your expectations.
> When you change your expectations, you change your attitude.
> When you change your attitude, you change your behavior.
> When you change your behavior, you change your performance.
> When you change your performance, you change your life.
>
> —John C. Maxwell[66]

More to the point, when you change your focus to Jesus Christ, He will transform your life!

Your Way or His Way?

During the early years of my wilderness wandering, I spent much time and emotional effort condemning myself as a permanently flawed individual. I spent little effort on learning to trust Jesus to walk with me across that foggy bridge and show me in His own perfect time the causes of my pain and difficulty.

As I began to peel away the layers of my life and understand the unsatisfied needs that had kept me stuck, I began to find healthy ways to get them met. As I became more aware of what I was thinking and feeling during stressful moments, I learned to make different choices. As I eliminated bad habits and conquered the fears that had controlled my actions and attitudes, I found it easier to establish new priorities and communicate more effectively with the people in my life. Then one day

I looked in the mirror and was delightfully surprised to discover a new Me that I never knew existed.

It was only when I finally allowed Jesus full entry into my secret room and shuttered heart that I began to understand His longing to draw me back to Himself and to respond to my lifetime of unanswered questions.

- Each time Jesus asked me to let go of something or someone I'd become too attached to, I learned something about His sufficiency.
- Every time He rescued me from a potential mechanical or financial problem, I learned something about His concern for each little detail of my life.
- Every time He asked me to trust Him with a complicated relationship instead of trying to figure it out by myself, I learned more about His faithfulness and wisdom.
- Every time I spent a night in tears, asking Jesus to please just hold me, I learned more about His intimate presence and comfort.

My only regret, if there is one, is that my stubbornness, pride, and childish naivety caused me to miss out on a lot of peace and joy that could have been mine sooner if I had chosen to stay close by Jesus' side rather than running ahead of Him and refusing to listen to His promptings.

Jesus wants you to let go of the "should haves." He might show you the truth about that experience that disrupted your life and damaged your psyche when He knows you're ready to hear it. Be patient! For now, He wants to be busy teaching you about the peace that is yours while you walk with Him through this thing called life. He's going to do that anyway, so don't fight Him along the way like I did!

Give yourself time to learn and change. Give God time to work! Trust Him to deliver the answers you need in His own time and in His own unique way.

Live and Learn

It seems I sadly misjudged
the course that life would take.
Running through thorns and falling into ruts,
life is full of questions, tears, and doubts,
yet sprinkled with a fair portion of peace.

I adore the One who loves and understands me,
who walks hand in hand at my side,
and carries me on His shoulders when I grow weary.

Walking and stumbling. Laughing and weeping.
I've lived and learned at the feet of the Master,
and I've chosen to walk with Him for as long as it takes.

By the way, there *is* one more question ...

Chapter 10

Do You Want to Be Well?

Believe it or not, there are people who don't want to be well in spite of the agony and confusion they're experiencing. When you're depressed, there can be some compelling reasons for staying stuck.

- You shy away from making new choices or setting boundaries because you believe you must please everyone.
- You fear setting boundaries, believing your friends will forsake you.
- You protest change and take refuge in the familiar. It's easier to make excuses.
- You don't want to look too closely at who you are because you're afraid of what ugliness you may find.
- You don't want to think about what you think about because it sounds like a silly waste of time.
- You don't want to examine your feelings because you're trying so hard not to feel anything.
- You are reluctant to let go of your anchors, your attachments, and all those things that have defined who you think you are.

I had become resigned to the belief that depression was my reality. Somewhere along the way, I had exchanged my childhood delight for a mind absorbed in shame and defeat. I had erected bold barriers to keep myself safe, and I mastered manipulative behaviors to feed my needs. I didn't understand that those barriers and behaviors I depended on to make myself feel better were the very things that were blocking my healing.

What Would Healing Look Like?

If you were to become fully well, would you turn into a stranger you don't recognize? Would you know what to do with yourself? Change can feel frightening, especially when you're uncertain what a new kind of life might look like. With healing comes responsibility, and healing would mean having fewer excuses for hiding and whining.

Do you defiantly cling to your shaming beliefs, your bitter attitudes, and your needy demands as you struggle to get through another day? Does it frighten you to think about making any significant changes to those thoughts and behaviors that seem to be your only defense against shame? Are you sure that you're ready to give up your dependencies in order to allow healing to take place?

My depression became a reason to beg for attention or withdraw from painful situations and uncomfortable relationships. I had missed out on some important opportunities to learn the life skills that are needed for healthy thinking and behavior. I learned that having a problem could elicit the kind of sympathy or personal attention I longed for. When I was consistently rewarded with extra attention, I began to use my depression as a means to acquire even more of that warm, fuzzy comfort I desperately desired. It also became easy to use my depression as an excuse to put off particular obligations or tasks that seemed too stressful or too hard because of my lack of basic life skills.

When it was first suggested to me that I should ask Jesus for help in working through my depression, I stubbornly resisted. Even though I'd known Jesus since I was a young girl, I had become consumed and suffocated by my depression, and my focus had turned inward. To even think about Jesus wasn't on my radar. I certainly didn't sense His presence with me as I painfully plodded my way through the "muck of melancholy," and I couldn't imagine why He would want to join me in my quest for answers. Too many others I'd counted on had already turned their backs and walked away.

Then one day while talking with Pastor Anderson about how discouraged and hopeless I was feeling, he quietly asked me this simple question: "Do you want to get well?"

I could have taken offense at that question, but I didn't. I was familiar with the Bible story in John 5 about the crippled man at the pool of Bethesda, so I knew exactly what Pastor Anderson was asking.

The Bible doesn't tell us much about that man at the pool. We know he had been ill for thirty-eight years. We don't know how old he was, whether or not he had a wife and family, or what kind of work he had done before his illness struck. He may have had some type of debilitating illness like polio, or multiple sclerosis, or Parkinson's that made him so weak that he was no longer able to stand or walk. He had been lying beside the pool of Bethesda for years along with other disabled people, including the lame, the blind, and the paralyzed. It was believed that when the waters were stirred by an angel, the first one into the pool would be healed. They never knew when an angel would come and stir the water, so they sat there day after day, hoping to be there at exactly the right moment.

I could see myself in those disabled people who longingly sat by that healing pool day after day. My struggle with depression had crippled me and made me weak and ashamed. I'd resigned myself to a life of gloom and had nearly given up believing there was hope for a better way of life.

In John 5:6, we read this:

> When Jesus saw him lying there and learned that he had
> been in this condition for a long time, he asked him, "Do
> you want to get well?"

What an absurd question to ask a man who had been disabled for thirty-eight years. "Do you want to be healed?" Huh? But Jesus doesn't ask foolish questions. He knew this was an important question for this particular man to answer. Why?

I wonder if that man had gotten stuck in his disability. Maybe he was getting something from staying by the pool. Maybe he enjoyed being around people who understood his predicament and provided him with some comfort. Maybe he liked whining to those around him that nothing ever changes and blaming others for his difficulties. Maybe he was earning some good money begging for alms and was putting it away in a retirement plan. Maybe he was using his disability as an excuse for not taking the fearful risk of moving a little closer to the edge of the pool. Maybe he had just given up trying.

Whatever the reason, this man had resigned himself to life as a cripple. He said he wanted to be healed, but to Jesus he only offered excuses. "I have no one to help me into the pool when the water is stirred. While I am trying to get in, someone else goes down ahead of me" (John 5:7). In other words, "I want to be healed, but I've done all I know how to do."

When you are dealing with depression or shame, you can easily resign yourself to the "same old, same old" weariness rather than taking the risk to move closer to the edge of whatever it is that frightens you or makes you uncomfortable.

Like that man at the pool, I'd been crippled by depression for so long that I didn't know what to do anymore. I was certainly hesitant to go back into therapy. I'd already seen several counselors over many years without any tangible results. When presented with any advice, I was quick to respond with, "Yes, but ..." I deliberately resisted any encounter with the red-eyed monster I feared the most: change.

Although it was in therapy that I gradually realized I had been clinging to my depression as if it were a lifesaver, I struggled to muster up the courage to become vulnerable to the probing questions and disquieting suggestions of my counselors. However, like the man at the pool of Bethesda, I had reached a breaking point. My depression had become so destructive to me personally and to my relationships that I knew I had to make a giant leap of faith. I desperately wanted to find some welcome light at the end of that long, foggy bridge I was traveling. Thankfully, I hadn't quite given up believing that Jesus may still be able to rescue me and bring me back to life.

Accepting Personal Responsibility

Although Jesus heard the crippled man's excuses for not making further efforts to find healing in the pool, He knew from the man's own words that he sincerely wanted to be well. Jesus simply said, "Rise, take up your pallet, and walk."

Seriously? This man hadn't walked in years! I'd be thinking, *You're crazy! That's impossible!* From a human perspective, such a thing was physically impossible. Have you ever seen the legs of someone who hasn't walked in years? The muscles are atrophied, and the legs have become just skin and bone.

The same can be true of someone who has been depressed for an extended period of time. Their social skills have become atrophied, their confidence has been weakened, and they've become emotionally paralyzed and unable to even dream of a solution, much less find the strength and courage to stand up and take a single halting step forward in the dark.

The Closed Door

It had been suggested to me that I try a newer form of therapy called eye movement desensitization and reprocessing (EMDR).[67] By the time I was asked, "Do you want to get well?" I knew I was ready to abandon my excuses and do whatever was necessary to begin moving in the direction of healing. I had resigned myself to the belief that EMDR was my last hope. In that quiet moment in Pastor Anderson's office, I reached out a trembling hand to Jesus and asked Him to help me take that first timid step toward the "end of the bridge." Ironically, that surrendering was the beginning of genuine, lasting change.

In one of the EMDR sessions with my therapist, I found myself wandering (in my mind) down a long, dark hallway, where I came up against a cold, heavy, steel door. I wondered what was behind that door and began to feel anxious, like a little girl on a strange adventure. Then Jesus arrived on the scene. I had my hand on the door handle, wanting to go inside. But I was so small, and the door was so big and heavy that I couldn't open it myself. I asked Jesus to open the door for me. He took my hand, moved to a chair by the door, lifted me onto His lap, and said, "Let's just sit here for a little while." I was content to let Him hold me— for a moment. I soon started squirming because I really wanted to go through that door. I kept looking at it and wondering.

Finally, Jesus quietly said, "Look at me."

I stopped fidgeting and glanced at Him, but again I turned away and looked at the door. "I want to see what's behind that door, Jesus. It might be what I'm looking for."

Again He said, "Look at me." When I looked at Him again, He asked, "Will you be disappointed if there's nothing behind the door?" I shrugged my shoulders and sat there quietly pouting. When I peeked over at the door again, Jesus asked, "Do you know how much I love you?"

Like the impatient little child that I am, I said, "Sure, but when are you going to open that door for me?"

Jesus tilted His head and smiled. "Look at Me, precious child ... Look at Me." I looked straight into His gentle eyes. Oh, the tenderness and compassion I saw there! He touched something inside my heart that had been locked away for a very long time. At last I understood deep in my soul that He loves me and knows how to soothe my pain and fill my need. He longed for me to take my mind off my fears, hand over my feelings of shame and inadequacy, and look to Him for the answers I was seeking.

When you make the decision to focus your attention away from yourself and other imagined saviors and look to Jesus, things will begin to change as you finally see the door to your heart opened wide by Jesus' soothing, healing love.

That's the whole point of this book! You can turn your life around by changing the way you think about not only who you are but *Whose* you are.

Are you ready to give up your dependencies on people and things and faulty beliefs so Jesus can make you whole? What comfortable attachments might He ask you to leave behind in order to experience His healing touch? Piercing questions like these can bring you to your knees. Then Jesus will ask: "Do you want to be well? Look at Me."

God is able through His strength to provide a way for you to escape any weakness of the flesh or mind, assuming you want a way out! We read these words in 1 Corinthians 10:13 (NCV).

> The only temptation that has come to you is that which everyone has. But you can trust God, who will not permit you to be tempted more than you can stand. But when you are tempted, he will also give you a way to escape so that you will be able to stand it.

The Greek word for *escape* used in scripture means to walk out of a trap or a place that's not good for you. This could be any weakness, from having a problem with anger to thinking poorly of yourself, to being afraid to take an honest look at your fear, to wanting to give up without first exploring your options. Satan is the master manipulator, hooking you into destructive habits, whispering his own putrid thinking in your ear, and leading you into a kind of hopelessness he has personally crafted for you. It's in your weakness that you must call on God for the wisdom to recognize the wiles of the enemy and seize the courage to run toward the open door Jesus is providing.

In Jeremiah 29:11–14, God has made this promise to all who are in captivity, whether captivity of the body, captivity of the mind, or captivity of the spirit.

> "For I know the plans I have for you," declares the LORD, "plans to prosper you and not to harm you, plans to give you hope and a future. Then you will call on me and come and pray to me, and I will listen to you. You will seek me and find me when you seek me with all your heart. I will be found by you," declares the LORD, "and will bring you back from captivity."

Grandpa, Part 2: Resolution!

Thoughts of my grandpa had been far from my mind since I was a teenager. That long-ago day in time that had brought life to a stop for me emotionally had been forgotten. As I entered my mid-fifties, I was a mess of conflicting emotions and beliefs about myself and was still experiencing persistent depression.

I'll always remember the moment when Jesus revealed the truth to me about that long-forgotten event that had sent me spiraling into depression. In a way only Jesus understands, He took me back to that day and place in time. I was standing in the living room of my grandparents' home. Jesus was kneeling right there beside me as I watched Grandpa being wheeled out to the dining room for lunch. In that distressing moment, Grandpa looked right at me, his first granddaughter, and began to cry. Jesus put His arm around my shoulder, snuggled up close, and whispered softly in my ear, "Your grandpa is crying because he knows he won't get to see you grow up." That declaration of truth finally opened the floodgates of my heart, and an ocean of long bottled-up tears was released. In the counselor's office, I couldn't stop crying as I finally began to grieve that long-ago loss of my beloved grandpa. In that moment of genuine grief, Jesus was able to begin the work of freeing me from the distorted childhood belief that I was at fault for Grandpa's "going away."

If Jesus decides the time has come to take you back to a particular memory for healing, it doesn't mean you will no longer remember the moment or the trauma. It only means that Satan's false message will be removed from the memory and replaced with the peace of God's Truth so the cruelly embedded shame from that moment in time no longer has power over you.

Today when I think of those last-remembered minutes with Grandpa, I still shed tears over the loss of that precious soul. However, there is no more confusion or guilt. Jesus is now an integral part of that memory. He is still kneeling beside me, telling me the truth about Grandpa's tears and filling my heart with the "peace that passes all understanding" (Philippians 4:7).

Just the Beginning

I wish I could tell you that being set free from the lies I believed surrounding Grandpa's death completely released me from the stranglehold of depression ... but I can't. I've continued to experience severe bouts of depression throughout my life. For a while, I pursued my agonizing search for lost memories or devastating traumas, but the search remained emotionally exhausting and unsatisfying as I ran from one closed door to another in the hope of revealing the prize which would set me free. Learning how our body chemistry can play havoc with our emotions eventually relieved some of my anxiety about "what's wrong with me," but there remained an underlying current of "not-okay-ness" that wouldn't release me from its grip.

Trusting in the Dark

There have been times when I thought God had completely withdrawn His comforting presence from me, yet more than once I've heard Him whisper, "You need to learn to trust Me in the dark." Even in the darkness, and sometimes especially in the darkness, Jesus has opened the door to my secret room and pointed His light into those hidden closets that had been forgotten or that I was fearfully protecting. It has been in those poorly lit closets and cobweb-filled corners where He has taught me astoundingly simple lessons that have cheered my soul and dramatically changed my focus. Jesus seems to do some of His best work in the dark!

In Matthew 11:28–29 (NCV), Jesus speaks these welcome words to all who are weary of the struggle.

> Come to me, all of you who are tired and have heavy loads, and I will give you rest. Accept my teachings and learn from me, because I am gentle and humble in spirit, and you will find rest for your lives.

Will you trust God for what you can't see, what you don't understand, and what doesn't make sense to you? Trust is like a muscle. The more you exercise it, the more it grows and is strengthened. Trusting an invisible God is not something that comes naturally to any believer. Trusting God in the dark does not mean that you won't experience fear or distress.

God is anxious to prove Himself trustworthy. One of my favorite scriptures is about trusting.

> Trust in the Lord with all your heart and lean not on your own understanding; in all your ways submit to him, and he will make your paths straight. (Proverbs 3:5–7)

How can you learn to trust God if you have nothing to trust Him with? The better you know Him, the more you will trust Him. The more you trust Him, the more you will sense His peace as you continue that wilderness walk through the uncertainties of life. If you're daily putting His Words in your heart, you will certainly recognize His voice when He speaks to you in the darkness.

Gentle Reminders

The Lord recently reminded me again of that icy confrontation with my dad when I was in my twenties. When I asked Jesus why He waited so long to reveal that disturbing memory to me, His reply humbled and thrilled me.

> I've always wanted you to learn to think of Me as your Daddy so I could draw you closer for instruction, for comfort, and for encouragement. You've been as reluctant and stubborn with Me as you were with your earthly

dad, but you've never given up calling on Me for help when the struggles of doing life overwhelmed you. Now you have a better understanding of why I gave you your earthly dad: to lead the way to Me, your Forever Daddy. You were able to catch frequent glimpses of Me in both your grandpa and your dad, and through their loving patience you began to understand how precious was your time with those gentle souls ... and how precious you are to Me.

It was your pain and confusion from the past that brought you into the shelter of my arms. I've had the sweet privilege that neither your grandpa nor your dad fully enjoyed of watching you grow and transform into the wise, funny, humble, and kind daughter and friend that you've become.

You've brought Me delight with your reluctant yet sure obedience as you've learned to listen for and respect My voice, heed My teaching, and trust My love. Both your grandpa and your dad are very proud of you, dear child—and so am I.

Forever Daddy

When you're in need of help,
His words are tangible and true.
He always keeps His promises
and won't stop loving you.

When you are feeling beaten down
by life, He'll be your joy.
He'll offer you a kind of strength
that nothing can destroy.

He'll stand by you and urge you on
when you don't want to try,
and when you fall, He'll raise you up

and teach you how to fly.

He'll hold you when you're lonely,
and He'll whisper in your ear,
"I love you, child; just rest in Me."
Then He will dry your tears.

When trouble overtakes you
and you long for sweet release,
He'll wrap you in a soft white robe
that covers you in peace.

There's no one else just like Him;
He's beyond imagining.
In this dark world of chaos,
He's the voice of sanity.

He'll stay with you forever
and will soothe away your pain.
He is your source of grace and joy,
your Daddy and your King.

Do you really want to be well? Jesus wants to heal your wounded heart and spirit. He wants to help you find relief from your paralyzing depression. How? You must seek Him out and, in His strength, choose to stop running from your pain. Confront your pain, feel your pain, and think about your pain as you begin to understand where it came from and why it lingers and robs you of peace.

If you're tired of feeling "less than" ...
open your heart to His love and His grace.

If you're weary of the constant struggle with depression ...
look into His eyes and welcome His peace.

175

If you're ready to learn new ways of being with people
and doing life ...
reach for His hand and ask Him for help.

if you're willing to trust Jesus and take a step forward
in the dark ...
then bravely do what He says.

In a particular scene of a movie (the title of which my aging brain will not allow me to recall!), I was deeply moved by the words of an elderly gentleman who was praying a blessing over the meal his family was about to eat. "Dear Lord, bless this food and the health of our family. For all the rest, we leave it up to you."

Are you willing to trust Jesus with all the rest? That's the kind of trust He desires. He can and will work in your life in sudden and unexpected ways if you're willing to trust Him with everything.

Now Choose Life

This life's filled with pain, and fears often oppress
and keep me imprisoned in so much distress.
I cry out, "Where are you, Lord? Why must I plead
for help?" Then He answers, "I know what you need.

"I'm right here beside you; I always have been.
You just haven't seen Me; your eyes are turned in
on the darkness of fear, shame, betrayal, and grief.
But I can bring comfort and blessed relief.

"I've waited for you to come closer to me
because you weren't ready to see what I see.
Now the time's come, and I know you'll be strong
while I heal your hurts with my own soothing balm.

"I'm here with you now, though you think you're alone.
I'll take all your sorrow and make it my own.

I'll hurt when you hurt, and I'll weep when you weep.
I'll guard and protect you, I'll watch while you sleep.

"There's no need to stay in the dark of your night.
Take hold of My hand and step into the light.
I'll be your safe refuge, your best hiding place,
your wonderful counselor, your Prince of Peace.

"It won't be much longer; it's not very far.
You know you can trust Me—you've done it before.
Remember the words of your favorite verses?
They speak about choices: life, death, blessings, curses.
Now choose life and move along to the next chapter,
and watch what I'll do to bring back your laughter.

"Cling to Me now, let My voice be your guide,
and My Truth will free you and hide you inside
the cleft of the rock, your fortress, your shield.
I'll nestle you under My arms as you yield
your fear and your pain to Me. Give up your strife
and learn to just trust Me—for I AM your Life."

Conclusion

So Many Questions ...

In the twenty-five-plus years that have passed since I first began thinking about this book, I've learned that life is much harder than I ever imagined! For most people who live in this broken world, even those with a sound sense of self-confidence and no serious emotional issues, there is a plethora of obstacles that stand in their way and prevent them from attaining their goals for health, freedom, and happiness. For people like me who have struggled to believe they have any worth on this planet, life can be painful and even unwelcome at times.

Do I wish I could have learned my life lessons without going through so many years of uncertainty and depression? Of course I do, but life isn't like that. What I know for certain is that although I've not yet totally defeated depression, I'm learning how to walk through it and not succumb to defeat. Is it easy? Nope. Learning to play the piano is much easier! However, learning to play the piano skillfully is a continuing process.

To play any instrument well, or to do life well, requires more than a handful of beginning lessons, a few weeks of practice, and a single good performance. You can't just say, "Okay, I've got it!" and stop practicing. There are always more lessons to learn, more refinements to make, and more techniques to master.

Your body chemistry and the daily problems of being human may continue to toss you into the muck of melancholy for the rest of your earthly life. Nonetheless, you can still focus your mind on the Solid Rock even when your face is planted in the miry muck.

Tailored for You

There's nothing new to be said about depression, but there's always something new to be said about the unique ways the Lord will work in your individual life. His answers and instructions are guaranteed to be tailored specifically for you.

Jesus knows how much pain you're in and how empty your life can seem. He understands it, and He's not afraid of it. Jesus doesn't see just your depression or your weakness. He sees the whole person He created you to be, and He has infinite ways to creatively and personally restore you to that state of wholeness in Him and show you His mercy, His grace, His teaching, His wisdom, and His love. He will show you exactly what He wants to teach you as you move through the bewildering wilderness of depression into the light of His Truth. Be willing to ask Him, "What do You want me to learn right now, in this time, and in these circumstances?" Then do what He says!

Perspectives will change, difficulties will diminish, and destructive thoughts will disappear under the tender, loving gaze of Jesus. His Light will shine where a moment before there was only dense fog and paralyzing fear.

Life is a long, maturing process. If you're paying attention, you'll discover that it is doing life that brings answers to your questions, fills in the blanks, and teaches you how to be. True recovery then begins when you start to face your issues, your struggles, and your brokenness with God's Word at your side. The Lord of life can lead you to the help you will need to keep moving forward through your journey.

Once you stop listening to the voices around and within you that are saying you're not smart enough, not talented enough, or not successful enough, and begin listening to the only Voice that matters, you will find His personal rendition of your song of life truly meaningful and delightful.

> Give God the freedom to work. Tell Him: "Do whatever
> you need to do with whatever part of me needs you."
> —Dr. Henry Cloud[68]

Disclaimer: The Master Singer probably won't teach you to play the piano. You'll have to learn that skill from flawed human beings!

Jesus may not tell you how long that foggy bridge is that you must cross or how many red-eyed monsters you may encounter along the way. Yet He can definitely be trusted to guide you safely to the other side! Along the way, He will show you some enchantingly brilliant views of peace and delight that you've totally missed before.

One Perfect Answer ...

> The Lord your God is with you, he is mighty to save. He will take great delight in you, he will quiet you with his love, he will rejoice over you with singing. (Zephaniah 3:17)

God Delights in You!

It's been my prayer, as I've written these pages, that you will hear the voice of the Singing God who can spotlight the true music in your soul.

Start singing with Him today! He can reveal to you the right notes, the right tempo, the right flats and sharps, and even the right time to turn the page so your song of life can begin to take shape and make sense to you. Your opening verse might be a dark dirge, it might be a chant of complaint, or it might be a lonesome lament ... but start singing! Jesus will honor all of your attempts to reach Him with your tearful tunes, and He will patiently dance His waltzes of grace with you, calm you with His lullabies of love, and bring you peace as He rewrites your song and lifts your spirit.

As you begin fearlessly moving forward on that foggy bridge with a song in your heart and your Maker, Daddy, and Redeemer at your side, He will show you the way from pain to peace, from depression to delight.

This is the day the Lord has made; let us rejoice and be glad in it. (Psalm 118:24)

Acknowledgements

Without the knowledge, input, and encouragement of numerous individuals, this book likely would not have been completed. Thank you to the individuals at Westbow Press, including Rebekah Cross, Joe Anderson, Tom McQuade, Jenny Alba, and Bob DeGroff who encouraged me to persist in the writing of the book, and the many staff members at Westbow who assisted in the editorial and publication process.

I have greatly appreciated the encouragement of many friends who pressed me to keep moving forward on the project. Three particular friends took time out of their busy schedules to read through several revisions. Thank you, Connie D, Kathy M, and Pam M for offering wonderful insights, ideas, and resources which were instrumental in improving the overall structure and content of this book.

Of course, without the prompting of our great Creator, none of these efforts would have come to fruition. I love you, Lord!

Appendix

Depression Survival Kit

TOOL	PURPOSE*
Can opener	**Open your mind to new possibilities.** Philippians 4:13 I can do all things through Christ, because He gives me strength.
GPS	**Listen for the still small voice of God.** Isaiah 30:21 If you go the wrong way... you will hear a voice behind you saying, "This is the right way."
Band-aid	**For life's little scratches.** Psalm 147:3 He heals the brokenhearted and bandages their wounds.
Dollar bill	**When you're running a bit short.** Philippians 4:19 My God will use his wonderful riches in Christ Jesus to give you everything you need.
Eraser	**Forget your mistakes and move on.** Philippians 3:13 I am still not all I should be, but I am focusing all my energies on forgetting the past and looking forward to what lies ahead.
Velcro	**Stick with it.** Romans 5:3-4 We also have joy with our troubles, because we know that these troubles produce patience. And patience produces character, and character produces hope.
Picture frame	**Reframe your thinking.** Romans 12:2 Don't copy the behavior and customs of this world, but let God transform you into a new person by changing the way you think.

TOOL	PURPOSE*
Clock	**Live in the moment.** Ecclesiastes 1:3 There is a time for everything, and a season for every activity under heaven.
Banana	**Peel away the layers.** Hebrews 4:13 Nothing in all the world can be hidden from God. Everything is clear and lies open before him.
Flashlight	**Shine God's light on your path.** Daniel 2:22 He makes known secrets that are deep and hidden; He knows what is hidden in darkness, and light is all around Him.
Whistle	**Blow the whistle on boundary violations.** Colossians 2:8 Be sure that no one leads you away with false teaching that is only human.
Blanket	**Covered in Jesus' love.** Psalm 91:4 He will cover you with His feathers, and under His wings you can hide.
Safety pin	**Pin your hopes to the Lord's promises.** Hebrews 10:23 Let us hold firmly to the hope that we have confessed, because we can trust God to do what He promised.
Teddy Bear	**Enjoy the comfort and cheer of a friend.** Psalm 94:19 When doubts fill my mind, your comfort gives me renewed hope and cheer.

* The Scripture passages are paraphrases of the original.

Endnotes

Chapter 1

1   Laura R. LaChance and Drew Ramsey, "Antidepressant Foods," *World Journal of Psychiatry*, published online September 20, 2018, https:///www.ncbi.nlm.nih.gov/pmc/articles.

2   "Donkey in the Well," http://syque.com/stories/discovered/donkey_well.htm.

Chapter 2

3   Michele B. Slung, *Momilies ... As My Mother Used to Say* (Ballantine Books, 1985).

4   The Myers & Briggs Foundation, "Personality Types," https://www.myersbriggs.org/my-mbti-personality-type/mbti-basics.

5   John T. Cocoris, "The Four Temperaments," http://fourtemperaments.com/4-primary-temperaments.

6   Fred Littauer and Florence Littauer, *Freeing Your Mind from Memories That Bind* (Here's Life Publishers, 1988).

7   Marcus Buckingham, *Now, Discover Your Strengths* (New York: The Free Press, 2001).

8   Tom Rath and David DeVries, *StrengthsFinder 2.0* (New York: Gallup, Inc., 2007).

9   "C. S. Lewis," https://quotefancy.com/quote/781638.

Chapter 3

10   Brené Brown, *The Gifts of Imperfection* (Center City, Minnesota: Hazelden, 2010).

11   1 John 1:6 NIV.

12 Although this passage has been attributed by some to Viktor E. Frankl, others believe that it was written by Rollo May, Thomas W. Galloway, or B. F. Skinner. Researchers have not been able to find this passage in the works of Victor E. Frankl. These words were popularized by Stephen R. Covey, but he has disclaimed authorship. https://quoteinvestigator.com/2018/02/18.

13 Esther Fleece, *No More Faking Fine: Ending the Pretending* (Grand Rapids: Zondervan, 2017).

14 Chris Tiegreen, *Why a Suffering World Makes Sense* (Grand Rapids: Baker Books, 2006).

15 Kathy Troccoli, "Stubborn Love" (Universal Music Publishing Group, 2008).

Chapter 4

16 Nanice Ellis, "Overcoming Negative Thinking – The #1 Cause of Chronic Depression," *Wake Up World,* 2019.

17 "Henry Ford," https://www.goodreads.com/quotes.

18 Marilyn Gordon, "Train Your Brain to Let Go of Habits," *The Mind Unleashed,* 2014.

19 Katie Byron, *Loving What Is: Four Questions That Can Change Your Life* (New York: Harmony Books, 2002).

20 Aaron Temkin Beck, American psychiatrist and professor emeritus in the Department of Psychiatry at the University of Pennsylvania.

21 David D. Burns, *The Feeling Good Handbook* (New York: Penguin Group, 1999).

22 Dr. Daniel Amen, *Captain Snout and the Powerful Questions* (Grand Rapids: Zonderkidz, 2017).

23 Compiled from Mary Whelchel's book, *What Would Jesus Think?* (Paris, Ontario, Canada: ChariotVictor Publishing, 1998).

24 Rick Renner, *Sparkling Gems from the Greek, Volume 2* (Tulsa, OK: Harrison House Publishers, 2016).

Chapter 5

25 Archibald D. Hart, *Healing Life's Hidden Addictions* (Vine Books/Servant Publications, 1990).

26 If you're interested in reading more about the "processes of attachment," there's an excellent book available on Amazon and through other book sellers: Gerald G. May, *Addiction and Grace* (New York: HarperCollins Publishers, 1988).

27 The amygdala is an almond-shaped structure in the medial temporal lobe of the brain that comprises a group of neurons. It plays a prominent role in mediating many aspects of emotional learning and behavior.

28 Jonathan S. Abramowitz, "What Is OCD?" International OCD Foundation, Inc., https://iocdf.org/about-ocd.

29 John Wilbur Chapman, "One Day When Heaven Was Filled with His Praises," 1910, Public Domain.

Chapter 6

30 *Rumpole of the Bailey*, a British television series created and written in 1974 by British writer and barrister John Mortimer.

31 Additional lists are available on numerous websites dealing with core values, including jamesclear.com/core-values.

Chapter 7

32 "Boundary," https://www.merriam-webster.com/dictionary/boundary.

33 Danielle Laporte, "The Difference Between Boundaries vs. Creating Barriers," *Positively Positive.* https://www.positivelypositive.com/2017/06/28/the-difference-between-boundaries-vs-creating-barriers/

34 Anne Lamott, American novelist and nonfiction writer. goodreads.com/quotes/24553.

35 Marsha Linehan, "Priorities Worksheet," *DBT Skills Training Manual* (New York: The Guilford Press, 2015).

36 Sherod Miller, Daniel Wackman, Elam Nunnally, and Carol Saline, "Awareness Wheel," *Straight Talk: A New Way to Get Closer to Others by Saying What You Really Mean* (Signet, 1982).

37 Bobby Robson, "Practice makes permanent," https://www.brainyquote.com.

38 Brené Brown, Ph.D., LMSW. *Rising Strong: The Reckoning, The Rumble, The Revolution.* (New York, NY: Spiegel & Grau, 2015).

39 Bill Gaultiere, *Your Best Life in Jesus' Easy Yoke* (Irvine, California: Soul Shepherding, Inc., 2016).

Chapter 8

40 Rick Ezell, *Defining Moments: How God Shapes Our Character through Crisis* (Downers Grove, Illinois: InterVarsity Press, 1990).

41 Carol Kent, *Tame Your Fears* (NavPress Publishing Group, 2003).

42 Tony Fahkry, "Why Guilt and Shame Carry a Strong Burden," *The Mission Daily,* mission.org, 2017.

43 Brené Brown, *The Gifts of Imperfection: Let Go of Who You Think You're Supposed to Be and Embrace Who You Are* (Center City: Hazelden, 2010).

44 "Shame," Jessie Sholl, "Shutting Shame Down," *Experience Life,* 2013.

45 "Sensations vs. feelings," Jessie Sholl, "Shutting Shame Down," *Experience Life,* 2013.

46 "Opportunity," Wayne W. Dyer, https://www.goodreads.com/author/quotes.

47 Brené Brown, *Daring Greatly: How the Courage to Be Vulnerable Transforms the Way We Live, Love, Parent, and Lead* (New York: Avery, 2012).

48 John Powell, *Why Am I Afraid to Tell You Who I Am?* (Chicago: Argus Communications Co., 1969).

49 The thoughts in this paragraph were compiled from a 2015 blog written by Leona deVinne, a leadership coach and consultant, https://www.huffingtonpost.com/leona-devinne.

50 "Eleanor Roosevelt," *Free, Fearless, Female: Wild Thoughts on Womanhood* (Minocqua, Wisconsin: Willow Creek Press, 2004).

51 "Trustworthy People," from "8 Traits of the Most Trustworthy People," *Power of Positivity, LLC,* 2019.

52 Brené Brown, "Braving—The Anatomy of Trust," creativebynature.org/wp-content/uploads/2018/01/BRAVING.pdf. You can also watch her TED talk on this subject at https://brenebrown.com/videos/anatomy-trust-video.

53 Henry Cloud and John Townsend, *Safe People* (Zondervan, 1995); Henry Cloud and John Townsend, *God Will Make a Way* (Thomas Nelson, 2002); Henry Cloud and John Townsend, *Boundaries* (Zondervan, 2017); Henry Cloud, *Changes That Heal* (Zondervan, 2018).

54 Brené Brown. TED Talk: *The Power of Vulnerability.* 2019 Brené Brown, LLC.

55 Terry Wardle, *Draw Close to the Fire* (Leafwood Publishers, 2004).

56 Chris Tiegreen, *Why a Suffering World Makes Sense* (Grand Rapids: Baker Books, 2006).

57 Kathy Troccoli, *Am I Not Still God?* (Nashville: W Publishing Group, 2002).

Chapter 9

58 Sigmund Freud was an Austrian neurologist and the founder of psychoanalysis. https://en.wikipedia.org/wiki/Sigmund_Freud.

59 Michael D. Yapko, *Breaking the Patterns of Depression* (New York: Broadway Books, 1997).

60 James Clear, *Atomic Habits* (New York: Avery, 2018).

61 David Burns, *The Feeling Good Handbook* (Plume, 1999).

62 Nathan Furr, "How Failure Taught Edison to Repeatedly Innovate," *Forbes,* 2011.

63 David Swartz, *Embracing God: Drawing Closer to the God Who Loves You* (Eugene, OR: Harvest House Publishers, 1994).

64 Jim Rohn, "Change," quoted at PacingOutcomes.com.

65 "Woody Harrelson," https://www.brainyquote.com/quotes/woody_harrelson_106060.

66 John C. Maxwell, *Thinking for a Change* (New York: Warner Books, Inc., 2003).

Chapter 10

67 EMDR Institute, Inc., "What is EMDR?" https://www.emdr.com.

Conclusion

68 Henry Cloud and John Townsend, *God Will Make a Way* (Thomas Nelson, 2002).